UNDERSTANDING MODERN ART

UNDERSTANDING MODERN ART - EXPLORING THE STRANGE & THE DISTURBING

JAKOB ZAAIMAN

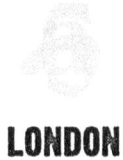

LONDON

Copyright © 2020 Jakob Zaaiman
All rights reserved.

ISBN: 9798666230626

Published 2020
Harfield Academic
London, UK

Cover art by Jakob Zaaiman

**This book is intended to be a simple &
easy-to-read guide to everything
you need to know
about understanding & appreciating
MODERN CONTEMPORARY ART**

It will set out in the clearest of terms
the principles of modern contemporary art,
so that you can properly evaluate and enjoy
contemporary artworks on their own terms.

Anyone with an interest in any of the arts
can read this book: you do not need to have an
advanced education, or specialist training.
We will also provide you with a very solid &
practical knowledge that you can
straightaway apply to each & every
encounter you have with modern contemporary art -
whatever the occasion & whatever the artform

(And for those who require scholarly detail, we have provided
footnotes and a bibliography.)

CONTENTS

THEORY

Introduction   3

Two objectives:
(1) an outline of the key prevailing ideas about art, leading to
(2) a clear definition of art and an explanation of its principles
Justifying an 'intellectual' approach to art – why should anyone bother ?
What will qualify as a 'definition of', and an 'explanation for', art ?

1   **Basic orientation: everyday ideas about art**   11

Art as 'paintings', and as 'historical culture'
Everyday art as decorative crafting
'Art' meaning an 'impressive skill', or an 'elegant solution'
'Art' meaning 'emotional expressivity'
'Art' meaning 'artforms', and the 'fine arts'

2   **The problem of a specific definition of 'art'**   15

Identifying the 'problem of art'
Possible solutions
Philosophical attempts at a definition of 'art'
Summary: drawing the threads together

3   **The historical background to modern art**   25

The evolution of the way we 'think about art'
Important idea: the emergence of the 'modern gaze'
The relationship between 'paintings' and the rest of 'art'
Important interim perspective: for most people, art is never more than 'circumstantial'

4   Types of crafted material   37

    Maslow's hierarchy of needs, and the idea of 'purposive crafting'
    Checklist of the basic forms of crafting, showing where 'art' can best
        be situated
    Discussion: the conceptual issues
    Example: impressionism vs socialist realism
    Summary: the main forms of crafted material

5   The conceptual trail from 'aesthetic craft' to 'art'   49

    The decorative aspect to crafting
    Aesthetic crafting and 'design'
    The concept of 'presentation'
    Da Vinci's 'Mona Lisa', and its experiential parameters
    Interim summary: utilitarian objects, presentational objects, and
        aesthetics
    The realm beyond aesthetics, namely 'art'

6   'Art mysticism', bohemianism, and creativity   57

    Problems with vocabulary
    Bohemianism, and creativity
    Modern life and its features: pursuing meaning and fulfilment
    The endorsement of 'high culture' by religion
    The secular quest for meaning through the arts: from the casual
        gallery-goer to the cultural gourmand
    The idea of engaging with culture as essentially 'worthy'
    Section summary: the array of forces contributing to 'art mysticism'

7   So then, what exactly is 'art' ?   67

    'Art' as an overall effect, not as individual standalone aesthetic
        objects
    'Art' has first to be 'curated' in order to become 'art'
    'Curation' as the moment something becomes 'art'
    Who qualifies as a 'curator' of art ?
    Any original creative intention can always be superseded by curation
    Interim summary: aesthetic objects vs art objects

8   For art to be distinctively itself, it has to reveal 'the strange and the disturbing'   77

    An artistic representation is not the same as reality itself: it is an abstraction away from reality
    Ordinary narratives vs artistic narratives
    'The strange and the disturbing'
    Interim summary: the conceptual trail from 'the beautiful', to 'the strange and the disturbing'

9   What do we want crafted objects to do for us ? And what do we want art to do ?   83

    Art as social and political activism
    Art as a 'spiritual calling'
    Art as 'unknown and unknowable'
    Interim summary: art can do more than confine us to 'the beautiful'
    The essence of art: presentational material which discloses and reveals

10   Problems with this definition: paradoxes and objections   91

    This is not a definition 'by decree'
    The theory that 'art' is part of a 'language game', and therefore has no fixed meaning
    The problem with popular usage
    So, then, how come this conception of art isn't more widely known and understood ?

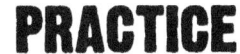

11   How does our new conception of art improve on the old ?   101

    Abstract vs narrative art
    Some of the extremes of modern art now make sense: Duchamp's 'Fountain' (1917), again
    Good and bad: successful and unsuccessful attempts at art

12 Examples of art: Bacon, Warhol, Beuys — 111

Francis Bacon (1909-1992)
Andy Warhol (1928-1987)
The concept of an 'artistic image' as an artificial persona
Joseph Beuys (1921-1986)
Summary: three archetypical artists

13 Examples of not-art: Emin & Hirst, Pollock, Picasso — 123

Tracey Emin (1963-) & Damien Hirst (1965-)
Jackson Pollock (1912-1956), and Abstract Art in general
Pablo Picasso (1881-1973)

14 Understanding Art: further considerations — 131

Art just isn't that easy to create
'Incorrect' as a (musical) genre
Activism and Political art

15 Gallery going: engaging with art & 'consuming' it — 137

Art criticism
Critical 'interpretative layering'
'Gallery-going'
Artworks as 'relics'
Artworks, and their display in galleries

16 Overview: art & our psychological life: where does art fit in ? — 151

Definition of art checklist — 155

Bibliography — 157

Index — 161

An important note regarding the illustration of artworks:

Given the resources now available to everyone, readers are far better advised to consult digital versions of artworks online rather than ones we could present printed on the page. Digital versions often allow for a much closer inspection of detail, as well as offering a wealth of other important contextual information. So at appropriate sections in the book we will alert the reader to connect with various specific illustrations online. And because many websites – even famous and important ones – regularly delete pages and change addresses, we will only give very general web directions, rather than links to specific pages.

However:
you will not need to consult the internet
to follow the arguments and discussions
presented in this text.

THEORY

All **aesthetic objects** 'aspire towards the condition of **music**' [Walter Pater]; and by the same logic we can also be sure that all **art objects** 'aspire towards the condition of artistic **narrativity**'.

Understanding Modern Art

INTRODUCTION

This book is all about how to understand the true nature of art. It will identify and explain– in the clearest and simplest possible terms – exactly what art is, what it does, and how it does it. Art is a major aspect of human culture, and it plays a crucial – if underappreciated – part in our everyday lives. Yet the various ideas of 'art' that most of us are familiar with are vague and contradictory, and hopelessly misleading when it comes to a basic understanding of what 'art' is in itself.

As things stand, 'art' is widely believed to be about trying to express, in some essential way, the aesthetic ideals of 'beauty', and 'crafterly skill and attractiveness'. And these ideals are meant to be realised by the application of traditional artistic skills and traditional art forms, of the sort that are taught in academies, schools and art colleges. But what has happened is that modern art has uncovered a whole new range of creative possibilities, and in doing so has mysteriously shifted the meaning of art away from 'aesthetic sensuality' and instead towards narrative realms of the imagination. In other words, art has gone from being about sensual pleasure, to being instead about exploring a very particular type of narrative.

Yet the artworld itself has yet fully to acknowledge this very radical 'change of nature', and so continues to interpret art in traditional terms. Art is still described as if it were the expression of 'beauty' and 'truth' and other forms of sensorial – meaning sense-based, or sensual – stimuli, when in fact its meaning has shifted into the narrative realms of the 'strange and disturbing'.

In order to understand art from the inside, and grasp its essence, we need to be able to follow the conceptual trail from popular ideas of art - and from the way people generally think about crafted items - to more illuminating and insightful perspectives. This will clarify not only how many mistaken ideas about art relate to one another, it will also make transparent each and every element of the conception of art we intend to replace them with. This method is designed to achieve a very transparent and uncomplicated grasp of what art is, and what it is trying to do, so that art can be properly appreciated on its own terms, without any uncertainty or confusion. This will not result in art losing its essential mystery and fascination, or its power to inspire the imagination, it will simply mean that questions like 'what exactly is art ?' and 'but is this art ?' and 'what's going on in modern art ?' will have been resolved, and one will be able to enjoy artworks on their own terms.

Two objectives:
(1) an outline of the key prevailing ideas about art, leading to
(2) a clear definition of art and an explanation of its principles

This book will pursue two objectives:

1) a clear grasp of the prevailing ideas about art, both popular and specialist, leading to

2) a lucid definition of art itself, with an explanation of its principles.

These two closely interrelated objectives are each as important as the other, and it is not meaningful to separate them. And if the reader is not sufficiently convinced by the definition of art which emerges in the course of the various analyses, they will at least have the consolation of having been shown all the elements that make up the established view of art, and will therefore be in a position to decide for themselves what still needs to be clarified and explained.

Justifying an 'intellectual' approach to art – why should anyone bother ?

We also need to offer a brief justification for the idea of an 'intellectual' approach to art. This approach will validate itself more convincingly as the book progresses, but we still need to emphasise its value right at the outset.

By 'intellectual' we mean an approach to art which is based on clarity of thought, and founded on a simple and lucid understanding, of the sort that can be applied directly and immediately to whatever is presented in the name of 'art'. This is to be contrasted with any approach that relies on 'feelings' and 'sensitivities', and which views art as all about getting into a certain semi-mystical 'arty' frame of mind, and then letting inner likes and dislikes take over.

We can explain this further. Many who are involved in art, or merely attracted to it – and this includes professionals and academics – like to think of art as something you simply immerse yourself in, and experience directly – in a kind of 'aesthetic receptivity', as it were – instead of as something you have to 'think' about, whether by having to 'explain' things, or by feeling pressured into pondering various 'meanings'. Artists have always associated themselves with loose living and bohemianism, embodying the belief that freeing yourself from the demands of any kind of moral and intellectual focus is an effective way of encouraging an appropriately sensitised 'artistic' mindset. So art is seen as psyching yourself into its realms, and then somehow residing there, maintaining the 'arty mood' by any means necessary. In 1960s terminology, art is about 'grooving', and 'digging it', and entering the right psychological frame of mind; and in this way the basic logic behind artistic receptivity shares many features with religious moods and mystical atmospheres.

We can even take the anti-intellectualism further and say that there is a hidden fear that 'thinking' – that is, ruminating, pondering, deliberating – about art might actually switch art itself off at source, and destroy any capacity to experience it fully. Art tends to be cherished for its sensual openness, and immediacy – as a kind of direct experiential availability – and is not something that you would want to approach through a 'cold and calculating' intellect. Art is widely felt to be the polar opposite of analytical and objective thought, and perhaps even its enemy.

Yet this is seriously mistaken. To know what art is, you need to understand it, and to understand it you need to be able to recognise it, and to recognise it you need to be able to tell the difference between 'art' and 'not art'. This isn't something you do mathematically, or by referring to a prepared checklist, but you do need to be in full possession of some clear ideas, and to be able to apply them with ease. And the conception of art which will be outlined in this book is very simple and straightforward, and easily understood.

So we begin by making it clear that there is everything to be gained in achieving a clear understanding of what art is all about, because this will tangibly enhance the whole encounter with art, and make the experience of it altogether more entrancing and immersive, and ultimately more gratifying and enjoyable. Understanding the principles of art does not in any way diminish the experience of art itself, or disempower it, or undermine it; in fact it does the very opposite. Of course we all know that there are many occasions where confronting a mystery, and subjecting it to the sunlight effectively puts an end to its mysteriousness; but this is decidedly not the case with art, because what we are dealing with here is not some delicate imaginary phantom, but an entire realm of experiential possibilities; and all these possibilities are currently being overlooked and disregarded by precisely the failure to clarify the basic conceptual ideas which are crucial to identifying them. In other words, people are missing out on the real 'art of art', and are putting up with a feeble substitute – a dismal 'second best' – and settling for that. Basically they are looking for art in the wrong place, and then refusing to give their disappointment any further thought, even though they have a strong suspicion that something has gone very wrong somewhere.

As things are, what currently passes for an engagement with art – especially modern art – is often mediated by the need to take on all kinds of dubious interpretative theories, and this in turn gives rise to a very real sense that insignificant trifles are somehow being dressed up as artistic treasure. No one seems to be able to offer a credible explanation as to what is going on, which leaves each of us having to cling on to random bits of 'specialist interpretation'. Not to have to think in these terms would be a liberation in itself, but we are talking about achieving an explanation of art which will have its own cogency, and its own substantial value, and is well worth attaining for its own sake.

To sum up: making the deliberate effort required to achieve an intellectual understanding of art does not destroy the experience of art, it enhances it. Art cannot really be enjoyed if you don't know what to look for. Without a clear understanding of what art is in itself, you have only your aesthetic prejudices and predilections to guide you, and so you are locked into something of a vicious circle, and most likely missing out on an authentic experience of art itself.

What will qualify as a 'definition of' and an 'explanation for' art ?

This might seem a somewhat peculiar question at this stage, given that one would think the answer is obvious, but the subject is not as irrelevant as it might look. Basically we are asking what will count as success in our quest for a practical and illuminating definition of art. And this question is directed almost entirely at the philosophical community, because, as we shall see, the philosophy of art – in other words 'art theory' – has been spectacularly unhelpful at shedding light on art itself.

Keeping it simple, we will break this issue down into its constituent parts. An 'explanation' is a formal expression in words of a cluster of ideas that help us to understand, and make sense of something, that may initially have presented itself to us as a mystery, or as an enigma. Explanations differ in their effectiveness, and usefulness, depending on the strength of our demands. Sometimes we are happy with a simple causal account of something; on other occasions we want to know meanings and relationships and implications. Some explanations undercut the significance of the phenomenon explained; others have the opposite effect, and end up turning their objects into an even greater source of mystery and fascination than they had to begin with.

We test our explanations by reflecting on them, and applying them to various facets of the phenomenon we want explained. Explanations need not necessarily reveal the inner workings of a mystery all at once, but for an explanation to be substantial and appropriate, it will somehow have to persuade its audience that, given time, it will reveal considerably more than it obscures. And it doesn't make sense for an explanation to be more complicated that the thing which it is meant to explain.

Explanations are usually grounded in definitions and distinctions, which serve to pinpoint various key elements of any phenomenon by formalising them in precise language. The various definitions can then be logically related to one another in a wider network of ideas, and the resulting conceptual scheme hopefully then serves as the basis for any relevant 'explanation'. The point about a meaningful explanation – as opposed to a specious one – is that it sheds light on how a particular phenomenon relates directly to ordinary life, and does so in a convincing way, without resorting to complexities. And the 'shedding light' – the explanation – has to validate itself by making one feel that one has a greater insight into an aspect of life than one had previously, otherwise there is always the chance that the explanation is no more than a clever-sounding form of deception.

Now when it comes to 'art', we enter into a peculiar situation. At the time of writing, there is no simple, easily understandable and widely held definition and explanation of art, yet the artworld does not seem to find this a problem. Artists create art, critics write their commentaries, and artworks have an eager public. In terms of a clear understanding as to the difference between art and not art, or between good art and bad, it is clearly a free-for-all. To justify an artist, or an artwork, you simply have to make a case of sorts, and the validation is sure to stand: there may be disagreements about the attractiveness and significance of the work, but not much about it 'qualifying' as art as such.

If we turn to the extensive literature on art, hoping for some help in understanding what art is all about, we soon realise that the principles of art – whatever they are thought to be – are everywhere implied, but never clearly explained. Artists tend to be declamatory about their calling, and seldom offer a systematic argument to justify their claims – which tend anyway to be based on traditional semi-mystical notions of 'beauty' and 'artistic expression', 'emotional truth' – whereas critics are wholly interested in writing entertainingly about their chosen topic, and are more concerned with anecdotes and local colour than with any kind of convincing theory.

Which leaves us with the academics, and their nit-picking conceptual ramblings; and these could hardly be less illuminating and useful if they were written in pure gibberish. The problem with recent philosophical attempts at defining 'art' is that they have focussed on striving for a very precise, quasi-scientific, almost paralegal checklist of attributes separating artworks from non-artworks, as if such narrow specificity would somehow also shed light on the nature of art itself. But the hunt for the 'necessary and sufficient' conditions for art has prevented more elemental and interesting lines of inquiry, and effectively turned the philosophy of art into worthless nonsense. In this regard, aesthetics in the so-called 'analytic' tradition is particularly disheartening[1].

So where does all this take us ? Basically to the need for an explanation of 'art' which will shed light on its essential nature, and relate it to ordinary life, without the need for academic complexities or artistic mysticisms. We know full well that the artworld can function perfectly happily and effectively without the least definition of art of any kind, nor is it particularly interested in looking for one, but our contention is that it is possible to define 'art', and to do so in such a way as to enhance the whole experience of art itself, and situate us 'art-lovers' in a more insightful position

---

[1] See how much more you know about art after browsing through Lamarque & Olsen (2004). 'Analytical philosophy' is an astonishing waste of time, and has never helped anyone understand anything.

than we were in previously. In other words, put simply, being in possession of a clear understanding of the most basic elements of art is a much more enjoyable and fulfilling, not to say insightful, position to be in, than being reliant on the confused and empty self-justifications one normally receives when trying to get an answer to the question 'what is art ?'

What we are arguing here is that 'art' requires, more than anything else, a definition which will not only separate 'art' from 'not art', it will also explain exactly what it is that art is doing, and what it is revealing to us, and how we can best understand it, so that we can appreciate it on its own terms, and make reasonable judgements as to success and failure, and the good and the bad. Otherwise we are condemned to remain in a kind of intellectual transit camp, unable to make simple and objective sense of the many challenging objects and experiences we encounter in art, and unable to come to conclusions with any real confidence.

To summarise: what we are trying to do is identify and describe a situation in which very basic and elemental ideas – such as a clear definition of 'art', and a clear distinction between 'art' and 'not art' – are clouded in mystery, yet this mystery, instead of bringing the artistic enterprise to a complete halt, is seen as a perfectly acceptable accompaniment to creativity and interpretation.

Understanding Modern Art

1

BASIC ORIENTATION- EVERYDAY IDEAS ABOUT ART

Art as 'paintings', and as 'historical culture'

If we are truly to understand 'art' – and the special role it plays in our everyday psychological life – then we also need to understand why popular ideas about art fail to do it justice.

And we can begin by identifying the different ways in which people think about art in everyday situations. This will show the variety of meanings of 'art' in popular usage, and why these ideas serve to confuse and mislead, and actually prevent people from appreciating what real art is all about. Studying popular ideas will not, of itself, present us with a definition of 'art' – or even point us in the right conceptual direction – but it will give us a feel for how confusing an unclarified idea of 'art' can be.

For most people, the word 'art' means different things at different times. This is not a problem as such because, at a push, we know more or less what we mean in any given context. It would only be a problem if we had to explain why we were using the same word to describe two different types of object, but this is not something we are often required to do.

Normally the word 'art' simply means 'paintings', or an exhibition of paintings. People talk about an 'art exhibition', and although this might be made up of various art forms, the designation, if unqualified, would lead one to expect a display of easel paintings. And 'art exhibition' also tends to imply the work of lesser known artists, as they would not be used to describe exhibitions of work by names such as 'Picasso' or 'Rembrandt', the idea being that everyone would already know what sort of work was involved.

'Art' is also often used to mean 'historical culture', as in 'the art of the Vikings', or 'the art of Native Americans', and in this context most people would understand 'art' to refer to cultural artefacts, perhaps delicately wrought and highly decorative, but not necessarily so. 'Art' here has a very different meaning from 'paintings', and although one might readily describe Viking implements as 'art', one would not call a museum of Viking artefacts an 'art museum'.

Everyday art as decorative crafting

There is, of course, 'everyday art' of the strictly decorative, visual variety: framed paintings around the house, bedroom pop art posters, and interesting ethnic knickknacks in the lounge; but these items are somewhat peripheral to the general thrust and drift of life, and once again are only accorded serious attention by 'artistic' types. Then, on a more elevated level, there's 'exhibition' art, from class assignments on school walls, to amateur displays of Sunday paintings in a local hall; and from museum collections in national galleries, to full-scale blockbuster exhibitions in major venues. Special events may attract crowds and hold interest for a time, and permanent museum collections will always draw a steady stream of visitors, yet both types of high end institutional art have only a narrow reach, and a limited appeal. And we also need to remember that, over and above whatever undoubted pleasure people may derive from looking at the exhibits, there is also a subtle if pervasive feeling that attendance at such gatherings is spiritually virtuous, and helps advance civilisation and culture.

This is everyday visual art in its conventional guise, as culturally worthy and – at least in some circles – decoratively desirable. There are also other everyday art forms which people engage with even more avidly, such as recorded music, television, video (in all its many types of 'screen' manifestations), and film. And to the extent that these are seamlessly integrated into everyday routines, people no longer even think of them as qualifying as art forms: they are just part of the ordinary fabric of life.

'Art' meaning an 'impressive skill', or an 'elegant solution'

We also use the word 'art' to mean 'skilful manipulation'. This is our most casual and non-technical use of the term 'art', though it still expresses an idea which carries over into specialist definitions, namely that of a practiced dexterity, showing itself in a kind of effortless elegance. For example, we might witness an everyday action which we consider sublimely executed or crafted – perhaps an expert sushi chef filleting a fish; or an experienced dealer shuffling cards – and we might express our delight and amazement at these moments of effortless technique by declaring 'Wow ! That's real art !' What we mean is that the display of technique has somehow transcended mere practiced proficiency and become something marvellous in itself, regardless of the mundane function it fulfils, and perhaps even because of it. And fully implied in our mental re-categorisation of these events as 'art', is the belief – even if we are joking – that they should be considered as of the same order as fine crafting, and skilled musicianship, and the like.

This conception of 'art' even extends to the idea of 'elegant solutions'. This is a way of recognising 'neat outcomes' to difficult situations. The way cupboards have been fitted, or kitchens redesigned, or plumbing installed, can, on occasion, seem 'artistic' in the cleverness of their execution. We seem to want to have a concept which recognises this, and which elevates the elegant solution into a special class of its own, above mere commonplace handiwork.

'Art' meaning 'emotional expressivity'

Many people also associate art and artists with 'the emotions'. Art is popularly believed to be about 'feelings' and 'sensations', and artworks are understood to be their 'expression'. Artists create artworks to express emotions – or at least instances of emotion – and the more an artwork can elicit an emotion in the viewer, the better the art, or so the theory goes.

This means that art is understood to be an activity and an experiential realm that people can participate in to indulge their feelings, and have themselves transported – albeit briefly, and in their imaginings – away from the emotional austerity of everyday life and the stresses of mundane problem solving. So an encounter with art is an opportunity for a kind of release, even if it is relatively subtle in nature, and confined to a response to elements of sensual awareness. In other words, it's a thrill of a sort, but not exactly something hallucinogenic.

'Art' meaning 'artforms', and the 'fine arts'

The concept of 'artforms', such as dance, ballet, music, opera, sculpture, theatre, cinema, video, and a host of others, would seem to indicate that 'art' possesses a specific nature of its own, which is expressed in, and through, various formal channels, or media. At first glance this might seem to tie in with the idea of 'art' as an elegant skill, practiced to a level where it becomes effortlessly magnificent, transcending the ordinary, yet 'art form' seems to bring along with it another dimension which is not contained in the idea of mere dexterity, and technique. 'Art form' and 'fine art' seem to be implying something more substantial and elementally characteristic than mere excellence of accomplishment.

And from these various meanings we can easily accept that the idea of 'art' has, in the light of the various ways in which it is used, already become unstable, and confusing. We have 'art' meaning paintings and decoration, alongside 'art' meaning skill, alongside 'art' meaning some kind of refined and formal expression. We have no problem identifying and explaining the different uses and the different contexts in everyday speech, but things get complicated if we start thinking in terms of a more generalised underlying concept which would supposedly cover all cases. And it is this underlying concept which is the crucial subject of this book.

2

THE PROBLEM OF A SPECIFIC DEFINITION OF "ART"

We now need to explain in some detail exactly how the prevailing conception of 'art' – in both popular and specialist circles – comes to be a 'problem', and how this problem actively prevents a meaningful understanding of the essential nature of art itself.

If we try to discover the nature of art by reading books on it, or by watching relevant documentaries, we will soon be faced with a curious fact: 'art' is everywhere spoken about, yet never meaningfully defined, or explained. 'Art' is always referred to as if everyone knows exactly what it is – in its guise as a secret prime mover, as it were – yet no one can describe its essential features in simple language. There are many books with titles like 'What is art ?'[2] and 'But is it art ?'[3] and 'Contemporary Art'[4], and 'Modern Art'[5], and so on, which one would think would eventually deal with the topic of a definition directly – and spell it out – yet they never manage to, and always sidestep the issue. It's as if packing a book with interesting pictures and 'authoritative' commentary on 'artworks' is all you really need to do, and 'art' will miraculously explain itself in the process.

Coffee table art books – large format tomes, filled with glossy colour pictures – are obviously good business, as there are any number of them in all

---

[2] Canaday (1980).
[3] Freeland (2002).
[4] Stallabrass (2006).
[5] Cottington (2005).

good bookshops, and they continue to be published with great regularity. If this tells us anything, it is that we don't need to be able to articulate a definition of 'art' to be able to join in the world of 'enjoying art', whatever that might mean, and whatever that might involve. It is enough simply to like looking at pictures, and going to galleries and museums, and watching the occasional 'art' documentary.

Naturally enough, the question 'what is art ?' does come up from time to time in public debate, and the topic can be relied upon to generate strong passions. All kinds of ideas are exchanged, many of them secretly but firmly based on the assumption that art is all about 'emotional expression' and the representation of 'beauty', yet the ensuing discussions invariably fail to identify any unique or decisive characteristics of 'art', and so eventually amount to no more than a statement of opinions. And for those inspired to take a serious interest in the subject – really wanting to know what 'art' is all about – the inconclusive nature of debates about 'what is art ?' confirm a very real sense that – whatever it might really be in itself – 'art' is so vast and indefinite that it is best just conceived of as an awesome mystery, beyond intellectual containment. This is where the idea of art as a form of secular mysticism comes in, insofar as art is believed to be something you 'feel' and 'immerse yourself in', rather than something you can meaningfully analyse intellectually.

Identifying the 'problem of art'

The idea of 'art' as a form of immersive semi-mystical experience is both very compelling and attractively believable, which is why it persists as a kind of subliminal doctrine. It has the clear advantage of not only putting an end to the need for any kind of formal definition, it also allows anyone's opinion of 'art' to be judged as good as anyone else's, though, of course, there is the widely accepted underlying belief that 'art' is about beauty, and skilled formal technique, and not about anything else. But on the surface at least, 'art' is talked about as if we are all free to make of it what we want, and that all ideas, good and bad, high and low, all go towards increasing our appreciation of this great creative and expressive process. 'Art' is mysteriously self-sufficient, and can well be left to take care of itself. So discussing 'art' is a complete free-for-all, and everyone is entitled to their particular opinion. Let's just enjoy it, and let it work its magic, and not think too much about it, is the general drift. But as it turns out, the more we strive for definitional precision, and the more effort we give to illuminating the exact principles of 'art', the more interesting 'art' itself reveals itself to be.

And there are also some very surprising discoveries along the way. We run into one as soon as we try to locate the exact moment at which 'art' changes from being something simple and straightforwardly understandable, and becomes instead something enigmatic and perplexing. We are talking here about identifying those situations in which our own use of the word 'art' is felt to be problematic, or uncertain, and we are not sure exactly what we mean by it, or what it is supposed to explain. This can happen in any number of contexts, but we are most often aware of it when we try to understand how modern visual art – in its most uncompromising forms – relates to traditional fine art, of the sort we see in museums and national galleries. How do bits of Joseph Beuys's 'found junk' relate to gold framed oil paintings by Rubens ? How do Jackson Pollock's splotches of paint relate to the technical majesty of Raphael ? The mismatch is so glaring as to be absurd, and even unnerving. Are we even talking about the same thing ?

So our implicit idea of 'art' as 'fine art' – meaning sophisticated and technically accomplished traditional artworks – just won't stretch to cover modern, non-technically accomplished, non-standard artworks, and this pushes us into a very elemental confusion, uncertain as to what is really going on. What could 'art' actually be ? What links the ultra-modern to the ultra-classical ? In fact, everything supposedly problematic about art begins and ends right here. So we can say that the 'problem of art' boils down to the fact that the ideas we use to appreciate traditional fine art – in all its forms – just can't make any real sense of modern contemporary art, especially modern visual art – and so our understanding capacity grinds to a halt.

And what is surprising about this discovery of the mismatch between traditional and modern is that it's almost entirely centred on visual art, and is much less of a problem when it comes to other art forms. It's the shock of modern visual art – paintings and sculpture – which has caused people to question the very essence of 'art' itself, and not so much the shock of modern music, dance, or poetry. You may not much like the compositional extremities of John Cage, or Gaby Agis, or of Bob Cobbing, but they don't exactly threaten their chosen medium with conceptual collapse. They have their own particular place in the grand scheme of things, and experimental works can at least act as a bracing contrast to more mainstream offerings.

Possible solutions

But if modern paintings and modern sculpture don't appear to have any meaningful connection to the classical tradition, how are we to evaluate them ? More to the point, how are we to enjoy them ? Are they really 'art' in the first place ? Do we just respond to our innate aesthetic 'likes and dislikes', or is there something more to modern art than that ?

Basically this leaves us with a series of options, none of which offers an easy way out. The most obvious solution would be to decide that only classical fine art is worthy of the status of 'proper' art, and that all else is failure. This argument has a certain surgical precision to it, resolving at a stroke the difficulties involved in deciding what 'art' is, or is not, by simply dismissing anything and everything which does not conform to the traditional; yet this kind of self-validating conservatism always runs the very real risk of failing to develop the capacities and sensitivities needed to appreciate new experiential opportunities, because it has convinced itself that there is no more to learn. And like traditionalist ideologies everywhere, it harks back to a distant golden age of seriousness and dedication of purpose, when painters had real skill and vision, whereas now everything is feeble and fake and slipshod.

Another possible way to integrate the traditional and the modern is to portray modern painting as requiring 'interpretation' before it can be fully appreciated. In this way, modern art becomes about 'ideas', and so you have to know what the idea behind the artwork is, in order to be able to understand – and enjoy – what you see[6]. This sounds perfectly reasonable in theory, and the logic of this perspective seems to explain away many of the difficulties viewers might be confronted with when they first encounter modern artworks.

But there are a number of inherent difficulties with this 'interpretative' approach, which is why it is always likely to arouse a certain amount of suspicion. At the most basic level, one can't avoid the sense – when attempting to understand works that clearly did not involve much physical skill on the part of the artist, like monochrome paintings, or readymade sculptures – that too much weight is being given to interpretation, and that the art itself doesn't deserve it. Or to put it another way, the viewer is having to do all the work, and the artist is not really doing anything. This doesn't sit

---

[6] See for example Acton (2010), Ward (2018), Heller (2002).

well alongside traditional art, where breath-taking technique is on display, and where the artworks seem completely self-justifying in their magnificence.

And this deep sense of suspicion is further compounded by the fact that many modern artworks rely for their effect on symbolism of the most obvious kind, and it's hard for the viewer to convince themselves that there's a hidden message in there somewhere. Consumer culture readymades[7] and installations are a case in point - as are artworks which reflect political and social events[8]; the images may be striking, but the effect is momentary, and ephemeral. Worse still, having grasped the apparent 'message' (or underlying meaning), what exactly is one to do with it ? Repeat it to yourself ? Ponder it ? That may well be the artist's intention, but this kind of didactic and hectoring element to it just makes art seem vaguely trivial, and hardly worth engaging with[9].

Philosophical attempts at a definition of 'art'

We need to say something here about academic attempts at solving the problem of 'art', so that we can make it clear that descending into complicated and highly technical conceptual analyses do nothing to advance our understanding. For what it's worth, academic efforts at a definition of 'art' might as well be directed at beings on another planet, given their complete inability to provide useful, helpful clarifications of any kind. Anyone hoping to gain an insight into 'art' would do well to steer clear of the 'philosophy of art', especially that of the analytic tradition[10].

The reasons for this are instructive, and salutary, as well as being somewhat disturbingly self-evident to everyone except philosophers. Philosophy thrives in complexity, and conceptual intricacy, in that it fulfils a genuine intellectual drive for theoretical convolutions for their own sake, regardless of practical considerations. Philosophers like to believe that the

---

[7] Warhol's Brillo Box (1964).
[8] Activist artists like Ai Weiwei (1957-).
[9] For example the works of activist artists like 'Banksy', which are really no more than clever visual jokes in the manner of newspaper cartoons.
[10] For example books like Lamarque & Olson (2019); 'philosophical studies' as scholarly impenetrability and mystification.

impenetrability of their formulations essentially establishes their value, and this is further confirmed – as they see it – by the difficulties outsiders have in understanding what professional philosophers are trying to say. Outsiders can't possibly appreciate the range and depth of philosophical analysis, so the thinking goes, because they haven't been trained to think incisively and with maximum intellectual penetration, so they stumble about in an ongoing cognitive confusion, unable to see anything very clearly, and making all kinds of elementary conceptual errors. Philosophers like to think they are in possession of a secret intellectual superiority.

This is all well and good as far as it goes, because, when you think about it, every profession likes to think that it secretly keeps the world going, and that without it, civilisation would collapse. But we're concerned about 'art' here, and about finding a way to understand it, and be able convincingly to identify it, and judge it. Complex, semi-scientific, paralegal sophistry is a hindrance, not a help, in this regard.

For example, take this definition of a 'work of art' from a university press text:

> 'An item that is a work of art at time t, where t is a time no earlier than the time at which the item is made, if and only if (a) either it is in one of the central art forms at t and is made with the intention of fulfilling a function art has at t or (b) it is an artefact that achieves excellence in fulfilling such a function, whether or not it is in a central art form and whether or not it was intended to fulfil such a function.'[11]

Later revised to:

> '"w is a work of art at t if and only if (a) w has form c which is a member of C and the maker of w intended it to fulfill a sub-set of functions f1 ... fn of F such that f1 ... fn are functions of c or (b) w is an object which achieves excellence in fulfilling a function in F" 1

> where: w is an artwork;
> t is a time;
> C is the set of central art forms at t;
> c is a member of the set C;

---

[11] Stecker (1997), p.50.

F is the set of functions standardly or correctly regarded as belonging to C at t;

f1 ... fn are members of the set F'[12]

It is clear from these ramblings that something has gone terribly wrong somewhere, and those who concern themselves with ideas like these are lost in space, with no chance whatsoever of returning to the mothership. This is not a complaint directed at any very laudable desire for precision and accuracy - and conceptual specificity - but such standards of excellence must always be in the service of something graspable and applicable, otherwise they are meaningless. A definition of 'art' that fails to explain anything, and is essentially so complex as to be gibberish is a waste of everyone's time.

Analytical philosophy 'art theory' [13] has come up with a number of definitional categories of art, including the 'honorific' (meaning objects accorded art status by a kind of consensual proclamation), the 'open-ended' (meaning the idea of 'art' is flexible and changes according to context, and so lacks a fixed definition), and 'classificatory' (meaning an understanding of art based on the way art objects are classified).[14] Classificatory definitions can be further specified into 'institutional' (George Dickie),' anti-essentialist' (Morris Weitz), 'functional and pluralist', and so on. Classificatory definitions appear to combine observation with theoretical analysis, but insofar as they fail to ground themselves in a simple understanding of art as it is embedded in everyday life, they lack the ability to illuminate our understanding of art in any concrete way, and end up always oddly ethereal and rarefied, as if those proposing them had no real interest in art itself, only in theoretical manoeuvrings. Of course were these machinations to shed at least some light on art they would be worth pursuing, but unfortunately they don't.

There are two major traditions in the philosophy of art, the analytic and the phenomenological, though neither of them is particularly useful when it comes to illuminating the nature of art in itself. The 'phenomenological' method attempts to 'describe' its way to the truth, by a very detailed presentation of what it understands to be the key features of 'art', whereas the

---

[12] Ibid, p.56.
[13] There are any number of academic books analysing and explaining conventional philosophical definitions of art; see for example Davies (1991), or Carroll (2000); slightly more accessible is Barrett (2017).
[14] See Barrett, ibid, Chapter 1.

'analytic' thinks it can uncover all things by a laser-like focus on word meaning and conceptual interrelationships. Phenomenology tends to be bloated and open-ended verbosity, entertaining to read but ultimately unsatisfying[15], whereas analytic aesthetics rapidly descends into the kind of absurdist so-called 'precision' outlined above.

Now the key problem with both philosophical approaches is that they are wholly dependent on implicit conceptions of 'art', and insofar as these conceptions are either faulty, or inadequate, it won't matter how much 'description', or how much 'analytical precision' you bring to the table, you won't be able to conjure up anything of value. As we have already seen in earlier paragraphs, our everyday idea of 'art', though functional in itself, is made up of vague and contradictory sub-concepts, and these sub-concepts will not resolve themselves through 'exegesis' or 'forensic analysis': what needs to happen is that a new and better conception has to be created, or put together, such that it substantially improves on the contradictions and confusions that have existed up to now. Put more simply, our current conception of 'art' – as a mixture of the ideas of classical fine art, paintings, cultural artefacts, and dextrous techniques – doesn't explain 'art', and doesn't give us the keys to understanding it, and so our most pressing and immediate task is to try to find a conception that will. Philosophy thinks that you solve this problem by analysing the conceptions you already have; we are suggesting that you have to formulate something 'new and improved'.

Summary:
drawing the threads together

Our widely-held, everyday conception of 'art' – covering all kinds of implicit ideas of skill and craftsmanship and cultural artefacts – falls to pieces when it comes to modern art. It can't explain it, or elucidate it, or clarify it, in any kind of satisfying way. Our everyday conception makes it look as if modern art has no connection to traditional museum pieces, and so we are left wondering if there is really anything at all which deserves the title 'art' in the first place.

The most popular solution is to denigrate modern art, and see it as

---

[15] See for example Harries (1991) and others in the same series.

some kind of slightly ridiculous aberration, a student prank, and not really properly art to begin with. This leaves the traditional conception of 'art' – as fine art museum pieces – intact and unopposed, which means that there is nothing really to explain: 'modern art' is substandard and illegitimate, and even with the addition of much justificatory interpretation still seems slovenly and unfinished and opportunistic.

      But this kind of extremist repudiation of 'modern contemporary art' ought, on the evidence alone, make anyone hesitate, if not actually reach for the alarm bell. Might there not be a conception of 'art' which not only explains what modern art is trying to do, but also actually make this realm of 'art' itself an altogether substantial and legitimate and fascinating experience in its own right ? That's what this book aims to do.

3

THE HISTORICAL BACKGROUND TO MODERN ART

The evolution of the way we 'think about art'

Before we can move towards the nuts and bolts of a substantial, easily understandable definition of art, we need to explain an important perspective on the historical background leading up to the key events which gave rise to the new possibilities of artistic narrative.

So this section is not essentially about the history of art, but rather about the 'history of thinking about art'; and in a very real way, this 'thinking about art' – as we are doing it here – is a relatively new phenomenon, and requires some historical context and explanation.

For example, we don't know - with any real confidence - how earlier peoples, in historically prior societies, thought about 'art' or , more accurately, 'creative crafting'. We can speculate, but we can't know for sure, because even if we had written records describing these responses from a previous era, we would still be uncertain as to the contextual details required to interpret them.

For example, if we imagine a caveman doodling with a stick in some mud, and accidentally drawing a wavy line which looked very much like a bird in flight, we can't know whether he would react with delight – at the amazing representational accident – or with alarm, believing the bird image to be the work of an evil spirit. We can't know if the cave paintings of Lascaux were ever viewed by those who saw them at the time as items of aesthetic beauty; or whether the representational accuracy of the animals was strictly in the service of some kind of magical conjuring ploy, to control their spirits and make them easier to hunt, as some have speculated. Of course the cave painters might have intended a combination of both aesthetic and magical elements in their work, but given how difficult simple survival was in those times, it is most unlikely that the primary purpose of the paintings was ever merely 'cave decorative'.

> **Illustration: the cave paintings of Lascaux. The French Ministry of Culture has a virtual tour of the Cave, and there is also an official website.**

What we are saying is that we cannot automatically assume that the creative crafting of historically earlier societies, and societies with different value systems from our own, was appreciated and assessed in anything like the manner in which we approach things now. The idea of thinking about a work of crafting in terms of its 'visual interest and appeal' – its purely aesthetic qualities – given the functional and utilitarian purpose of most crafted items, would likely have been a very minor element in the encounter with the work as a whole, and certainly far distant from the kind of detached, recreational enjoyment we might associate with visits to museums and galleries today.

All of which means that if we are to understand art in any depth, we need to understand – at the outset – that the way we have of looking at artworks in the secularised, leisured society we now live in today is likely to be very different from the ways of appreciating and judging crafted works in other societies, and at other times in history. This is particularly important when we come to the phenomenon of modern art, which cannot really be understood if we are unable to appreciate the extent to which creative crafting in our society has become a form of recreation and entertainment, and is no longer functionally magical, or mystical, or religious in the first instance.

Important idea:
the emergence of the 'modern gaze'

So far we have noticed – in passing – that 'art' really becomes a problem only (or at least, mainly) when we try to integrate the exacting demands of classical fine crafting with the apparent slipshod lawlessness of modern art. If there were no 'modern art', classical art forms, from music to dance to poetry, would be relatively unproblematic. Classical art forms, as familiar features of human experience, possess a certain self-evident integrity, in the sense that they don't cry out for 'explanation', or 'justification', any more than, say, 'sport', or 'entertainment' do. Academic theoreticians could speculate as to how best to describe various artistic properties, and how these properties might best be conceptually related to one another, but none of these speculations would be urgent or decisive, and they would have almost no bearing on the exercise of the art forms themselves.

Modern art has changed all that. Modern art has made it seem as if chunks of wholly unrelated material are being lumped together in a highly implausible relationship, and we the audience are being forced to go along with this, having been 'told by the experts' that what we are being shown is all about 'interesting ideas' and 'interesting interpretations', despite the evidence of our own eyes. And when assessed in terms of classical technique, modern art looks completely shoddy and amateurish, and any attempts by supposed art professionals to argue otherwise just seems to make matters worse. People feel they are being treated as fools. How did we get into this apparent madness, and how do we get out of it ?

The history of the evolution of modern art is, as one might expect, closely tied to the evolution of our modern 'sense of self,' and our contemporary understanding of what life is supposed to 'consist of'. Modernity is essentially about the shift – thanks to technological advancement – from a life of more or less total oppression and drudgery, to a life with considerable scope for leisure, in which people have time to think beyond the demands of survival. And with greater freedom comes the desire to explore, and to experiment and to reflect; at least, it does in materially advanced societies.

The precise historical moments to which various important societal changes can be traced do not concern us here; nor do we need to be particularly accurate with regard to the interplay between the many and various historical forces: we can leave all that to the specialist historians. What is important for us is to achieve a very real sense of the way in which modern art has emerged from the constraints of the past, and how it has come to reflect and embody the needs that people feel have arisen from a whole new range of life possibilities afforded them by technological progress.

According to the history books, we can trace the first signs of the modern movement in art back to 'Impressionism' in France in the late 19th century, and to painters of that era such as Édouard Manet, and Gustave Courbet. Once again, it is not the specific details of the artworks themselves which is crucial – regardless of their historical importance in the sequence of events – it is the fact that they broke with tradition, opening the way for further experimentation and exploration.

We can outline the key historical events through quotes from various standard texts on art history. This from Arnason (2012):

> 'Various dates have been proposed for the birth of modern art. The most commonly chosen, perhaps, is 1863, the year of the Salon des Refusés in Paris, where Édouard Manet first showed his scandalous painting *Déjeuner sur l'herbe*. But other and even earlier dates may be considered: 1855, the year of the first Paris Exposition Universelle (a kind of world's fair), in which Gustave Courbet (1819—77) built a separate pavilion to show The Painter's Studio; 1824, when the English landscapists John Constable and Richard Parkes Bonington exhibited their brilliant, direct-colour studies from nature at the Paris Salon (an annual exhibition of contemporary art juried by members of the French Academy); or even 1784, when Jacques-Louis David (1748-1825) finished his *Oath of the Horatii* and the Neo-classical movement had assumed a position of dominance in Europe and the United States.
>
> Each of these dates has significance for the development of modern art, but none categorically marks a completely new beginning. For what happened was not that a new outlook suddenly appeared; rather, a gradual metamorphosis took place in the course of a hundred years. It embodied a number of separate developments: shifts in patterns of patronage; in the role of the French Academy; in the system of art instruction; in the artist's position in society. The period under discussion was one

of profound social and political upheaval, with bloody revolutions in the United States and France and industrial revolution in England. Artists are, like everyone else, affected by changes in society—sometimes, as in the case of David or Courbet, quite directly. Social changes lead inevitably to changes in attitudes toward artistic means and issues -toward subject matter and expression, toward the use of colour and line, and toward the nature and purpose of a work of art and the role it plays vis—a—vis its diverse audience.'[16]

And this from Hunter and Jacobus (1992):

> 'It has even been persuasively argued that the origins of 20th-century art go back as far as the 1750s. when 18th-century scientism and sentiment combined to initiate an aesthetic rehabilitation that would gradually replace elaborate Rococo artifice with soberer form and a greater sincerity of feeling. A more obvious and frequently cited point of departure is that brought by the French Revolution which shattered the *ancien regime* and rapidly accelerated the process whereby artists would be emancipated from the strictures imposed by traditional authority and left to paint as they wished, while often starving until a new system of patronage could emerge, consisting of the commercial galleries, private collectors, and public museums that we know today.
>
> Even more frequently advanced as the chronological beginning of modernism in the visual arts is 1855. the year of the Paris Exposition during which Gustave Courbet laid a solid foundation for the new patronage by building his own pavilion and there displaying such grandly iconoclastic works as The Painter's Studio. Equally important is the year 1863, when the Emperor Napoleon III allowed a Salon des Refusés to take place, in response to the appeals of artists working in ways unacceptable to the official Salon and yet desperate for Salon exhibition, since such exposure offered the period's sole means by which artists could hope for significant recognition and revenue from sales.

---

[16] Arnason (2012), p.1 ff.

Among the more than 2,500 submissions that had failed to measure up to the academic standards set by the jury was Manet's *Luncheon on the Grass*, the most innovative canvas to be seen and the focus of the most unbridled ridicule that transformed the Refusés into a three-ring circus, attended on a Sunday by as many as 4,000 curiosity-seekers.

Eleven years later, in 1874, the modernist movement made its next decisive inroad into Western consciousness when, once again, the conflict between the values of the French art establishment and those of younger artists ignited a rebellion. Although the Napoleonic monarchy had collapsed, as a consequence of the French defeat in the Franco-Prussian War of 1870, it had been replaced by a republican government scarcely less conservative than that of the preceding Second Empire. Scorning such officialdom, rather than pleading with them, certain progressive painters of Paris pooled their resources and mounted their own exhibition in the studio of the commercial photographer Felix Nadar. This was the famed show that brought before a largely derisive public a small group of artists whose fresh, freely brushed pictures so shocked a reactionary critic that he called the painters mere "Impressionists," to suggest their deliberate and thus all the more contemptible lack of finish. Here, indisputably, were many of the earmarks of the modernism that we have come to know in our own time: boldly independent art independently presented by a beleaguered band of self-confident innovators, scandalized press and public, and the coining of an "ism" to designate a certain radical kind of form.

However, for present purposes.... we have chosen to begin our narrative in 1886, after the last of the eight Impressionist exhibitions in Paris and with the birth of the Independents Salon. By then Impressionism, in its original form as an extension of 19th-century Realism or Naturalism, had run its course and entered a period of crisis, generating a new, essentially antinaturalistic wave of modernism—not only painting but also a body of theoretical writing to support it—upon which Matisse and Picasso, those twin fathers of 20th-century art, would base their own revolutionary and liberating procedures.

So rich and varied was this seminal fin-de-siècle period, which ran generally from the mid- 1880s to the advent of Fauvism in 1905, that since 1910 the term most often used to identify it has been the all-embracing "Post-Impressionism.'" [17]

[As a brief aside, we should mention that, although the emergence of modernism in art is now commonly accepted to be all about painting in Paris in the late 19th century, there is plenty of evidence of a popular depiction of modern, worldly sensibilities in the caricatures of Gillray, Hogarth and others in 18th century London[18], a good hundred years before the cultural scandals that overtook Paris. Whether or not it is possible to connect these two movements is something for scholars to look at, but there was clearly a drift towards a more secularised art, depicting common features of everyday life, in both countries.]

> **Illustrations: it is worth checking out the works of caricaturists such as James Gillray (1756 -1815) and William Hogarth (1697-1764) to see depictions – albeit as satire – of a highly secularised modern sensibility, predating French modernism by at least a hundred years. And this satirical type of secularised imagery of course has antecedents in Pieter Breugel (1525-1569) and Hieronymus Bosch (?-1516).**

Now although the historical particulars can make for interesting reading, and tracing the interplay between the various events has its own fascination, it is the fact of the birth of modernism which is key, not the exact details of its circumstance. And to push the point even further, it is not even the manner in which paintings expressed their modernity which is of interest, rather it is the fact that there was a very real sense that the strictures of orthodox methods no longer allowed artists to feel that they could adequately

---

[17] Hunter et al (1992), p.9 ff.
[18] See for example, Bills (2006).

express themselves, and so they began to explore new forms of composition and technique. And that this desire for experimentation was genuine and substantial is verified by the fact that it did not grind to a halt and fade away after a brief period of initial enthusiasm, but continued to involve into the modern art we have today, bringing with it entirely unforeseen experiential possibilities.

What we are talking about here is the identification, in historical terms, of the coming together of various important factors which led to the emergence of modern art. These factors are primarily to do with the possibilities that came with a certain type of lifestyle, which itself was the result of changes in the way society maintained itself. It may be tempting simply to attribute all these changes to the industrial revolution, but comparative studies of non-western societies may not necessarily show that industrialisation will inevitably lead to major changes in what society wants to do with its art, so there have to be other factors at play – such as a very specific form of western 'individualism' – which accounts for the trajectory of western European modernism.

Also – and this muddies the waters considerably – at about the same time as modern art was starting to emerge, Marxist critiques of society were being formulated, and these portrayed industrialised society as both morbid and constraining, and certainly not conducive to the kind of free spiritedness required for artistic experimentation. But we don't have to be able to explain the sociological dynamics to know that artistic experimentation succeeded in the long run, and that despite the negative aspects of industrialisation, it also granted some individuals new opportunities.

What can we say about the 'dynamics' which gave rise to modern painting ? We know that the early exhibitions of the new artworks were scandalous social events, likely attracting hordes of thrill seekers and the curious, but this kind of sensationalism would not have sustained anything in the long run if it was not expressing a genuine and substantial need. Artists themselves must have sensed, very early on in the process of their abandoning of academic restrictions, that there was much that they could explore, and that these explorations could, if all went well, last indefinitely.

Now in terms of the conceptual trail being followed in this book, we are tracing the emergence of a new type of creative expression, alongside the concurrent emergence of a new way of looking at creative craftworks. Artists were freeing themselves from the constraints of classical techniques, form and subject matter, and onlookers were starting to view artworks as objects of visual sensation and enjoyment rather than as items of cultural and moral worth. It marks a crucial shift from a kind of didactic and edifying aesthetics to a purely recreational one.

To summarise: painters gave us 'modernism', and modernism allowed us to view paintings as visual pleasures for their own sake. Paintings were no longer religious or mystical objects; they had become merely an expression of the desire to express. In this way, modernism gave us the 'modern gaze'.

The relationship between 'paintings' and the rest of 'art'

We need to remind ourselves at this stage that what we are trying to do, ultimately, is discover whether or not there is a 'something' – a distinct, identifiable phenomenon – which meaningfully links all the disparate activities and creations which, for whatever reason, are often categorised under the label of 'art'. The word 'art' as used in popular culture usually means 'creatively and imaginatively crafted', and is applied to objects and events and creations which are mainly produced for 'their own sake' – that is, for their recreational enjoyment – rather than for any utilitarian purpose. But this definition is very vague, and never quite identifies 'the something' which 'explains' what art is supposed to be trying to achieve, and so is not much help when it comes to understanding art in any meaningful way. This then simply leaves people alone with their own aesthetic prejudices and predilections, and the whole idea of 'art' remains somewhat mystical and mysterious, as well as very subjective.

Coincidental with the evolution of modernism in painting, modernism also took hold in the other art forms, such as music, dance, sculpture, and all the rest. Once again, the details of the causal interrelationships between the various evolving art forms are not our concern, though it is obvious that the desire for experimentation and exploration was widespread in the arts, and reflected a very real sense in which creative crafting was throwing off the constraints of tradition, and turning into something with its own distinctive nature .

So if we appear to be concentrating at this stage on the visual arts, to the exclusion of other art forms, it is only because the history of the visual arts offers the clearest and simplest conceptual trail to follow, without the need to resort to obscure and complex historical material. But underlying our exploration of the history of the visual arts is the search for a definition of 'art' which would make sense of **all types of creative crafting**, from the most grossly physical – like a metal sculpture - to the most cerebrally ethereal – like some kind of bizarre theatrical non-performance 'happening'.

Important interim perspective: for most people, art is never more than 'circumstantial'

An important but unseen - and therefore neglected - element in our whole enquiry is the fact that, despite the ubiquity of creative crafting in all aspects of modern life, from supermarket layouts to business branding, most people do not spend much time 'thinking about art'. People might like to feel they have an alert sense of fashion and design, and can tell the difference between taste and tastelessness, and good and bad art, but these are not subjects which ordinary people obsess about at any length, other than very occasionally. This is not meant to be a criticism of popular culture, but rather a simple statement of fact, borne out by the evidence of media coverage, and the generally very superficial way in which creative crafting of all kinds is critically assessed: it's always presented as being a matter of instant 'likes and dislikes', and not much more.

There is also an element of diktat in visual fashion, in the sense that 'today's look' is handed down to us from designers and trendsetters and window dressers, and we are simply swept along by the uptake. And although we would be mortified if the decorative element of our lives were taken away from us - and we were forced to live in a Stalinist monochrome - we treat our lived environment with a certain measure of casual acceptance, and we wait to see what the future will present us with. This is especially true of city dwellers, who might like to think they are protecting themselves with conservative planning regulations, but in truth they are at the mercy of all kinds of visually dynamic creative forces, and can find their neighbourhoods radically altered over time.

All of this is simply to say that, despite the intensity of the visual pleasure people may get from their elaborately crafted visual environment, they don't actively participate in it, beyond a very limited involvement. Creative crafting is something that the professionals do, and the rest of us await to see what they come up with. Art may be fun, but for most people it's just not that important, and is very much peripheral - circumstantial - to the demands of daily life.

Of course this is always open to change, especially if technology can deliver us more leisure time, as well as encouraging people to be more active in the crafting of their immediate surroundings.

Understanding Modern Art

4

TYPES OF CRAFTED MATERIAL

This chapter approaches the question of 'art' from a slightly unusual angle, framing it in terms of the types of purposeful/purposive crafting that human beings engage in as part of maintaining or enhancing everyday life. This may seem somewhat distant from what might normally be considered the key conceptual issues, but framing it in this way forces us to see 'art' for what it is, shorn of sentimentality and mysticism and confusion. This is 'art' as we encounter it in its most elemental relationship to human life: art as it is 'in itself'. This is 'art' before it becomes distorted by ideas of 'art mysticism' or 'artiness' or 'art consciousness' – immersive states of mind that one can will oneself into – because it is these fanciful ideas which prevent us from conceptual clarity, and which give rise to the mistaken idea that art is all about feelings and intuitions[19], and that you don't need to clarify your thoughts about it, or understand its principles, to know what 'art' is.

If we reduce crafting to its most basic categories, we discover that life is a lot less differentiated and open-ended than we might ordinarily think it is. We conceive of everyday life as full of very different activities and purposes, even if they are routine, but the differentiation is very much on the surface,

---

[19] Reaching a mystical climax as a 'disruptive' aesthetic experience, see Kuspit (2008) Chapter 1.

and seemingly very different activities can be meaningfully lumped into a mere handful of categories without distorting their essential nature, and without our being needlessly reductionistic. Food, for example, can be presented in any number of ways, shapes and forms, but in one sense it is only 'bodily fuel', and we do not distort its essential nature if we categorise it as such. And in a way we get to understand it better, provided we can balance an understanding of the open-ended possibilities of food preparation and enjoyment – the experience of food – with that of a more scientific conception of food as a crucial fuel – the elemental principle of food.

In fact it is this attempt to strike a balance between 'principle' and 'experiential diversity' – with regard to 'art' – which is the basis of this book, and, in real terms, is the key to 'understanding' and 'grasping' more or less anything. An appreciation of experiential diversity is one thing, but it remains superficial if it cannot convincingly be related to an understanding of the principles – that is to say, to the key elements, shorn of distorting sentimentality and anything extraneous and unnecessary – which ultimately have given rise to that diversity.

Put simply: to 'understand' something, you need to have a clear idea as to the relationship between *principle* and *diversity in practice*. You have to have a grasp of both the key elements underpinning a phenomenon, as well as a familiarity with the way that phenomenon manifests itself in various ways. Knowledge of the details is not enough; you need to be able to get to the point behind the detail.

So what do we mean by 'craft', or 'crafting' ? We mean here the deliberate modification, or manipulation, by a human being, of any kind of object, be it physical, like metal or a wood, or conceptual, like words or ideas, in the service of some kind of specific purpose. Sometimes the crafting can be so slight as to be almost imperceptible – for example simply picking up a lump of rock to use as a hammer – and sometimes the crafting is huge, as in the construction of intricate machinery. 'Crafting' is the process of deliberate modification of objects and spaces and ideas by humans in their external and lived environment. We craft the world around us to suit our purposes.

And as with the example of food, it would seem that, given the open-ended number of objects available to us to modify, or craft to our purposes, it would be futile, as well as uninformative, to try and list every possible instance of crafting. However, if we reduce the diversity to elemental categories such as 'purpose' and 'use', we discover an underlying interconnection between seemingly unrelated objects, and in so doing gain greater insight into the experience of life itself. It is the progressive grasping of basic principles which constitutes 'real understanding', not an increase in a knowledge of various details. In other words, it is the grasping of underlying principles – as a consequence of, and as part and parcel of, experience itself – which is important, not simply the ability to experience something – whatever it might be – more extensively. And, paradoxically, the more you understand the principles of what you are doing, the more intensively you are able to experience the manifold variety, because you are able to focus on the essential, and disregard the distractions.

Now when it comes to crafting, we can soon see that beneath the diversity, human beings craft objects for a surprisingly limited number of purposes. Most crafted objects are simply 'tools' of one kind or another; that is, items designed to facilitate the maintenance of ordinary, everyday life: implements for eating, sleeping, shelter, safety, and so on. And beyond basic items for survival and maintenance, we craft tools for what we believe will enhance our experience of our lives, from musical instruments to ideologies, and any number of objects in between.

Maslow's hierarchy of needs, and the idea of 'purposive crafting'

The relationship between the types of crafting that we might engage in, and the kinds of purposes we feel are crucial to our lives, can be informatively illustrated by reference to Maslow's hierarchy of needs[20], which is itself a valuable example of 'principial thinking'; that is, clarifying the principles underpinning a phenomenon.

Maslow proposed that human needs could meaningfully be understood in terms of a sequential hierarchy, contained in a pyramid, beginning with elemental physiological needs at the base, and ending up the scale with more cerebral needs such as 'self-actualisation' at the apex. Basic needs have to be taken care of before needs higher up the scale could be entertained, and this can be illustrated by the truism that you can't really move on to doing anything else if you are weak with hunger and thirst, so satisfying

---

[20] See Maslow (1943).

these basic physiological needs is a prerequisite for whatever else might be necessary in life. And having eaten, you then need to think in terms of physical security, and a safe environment. And having secured that, you can then think in terms of engaging meaningfully with the people around you, and so on. And having eventually taken adequate care of these more primordial needs, you can start to think in terms of how best to live your life.

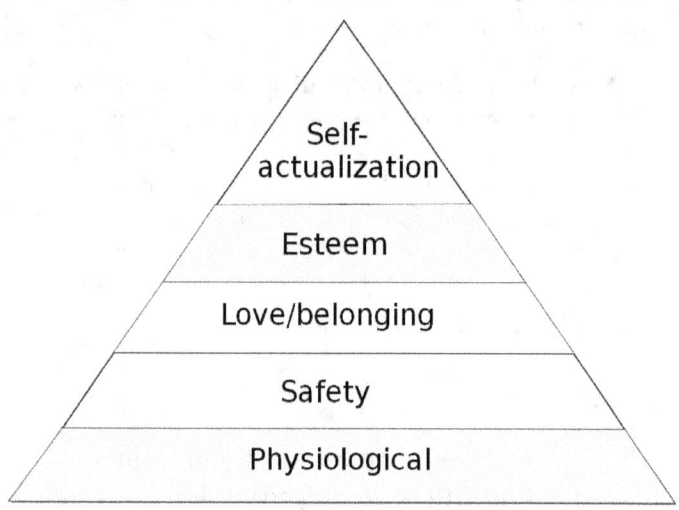

Maslow's hierarchy of needs

Maslow's hierarchy has something satisfyingly self-evident about it, once it has been understood, and it seems to identify an underlying structure to the bewildering diversity of human behaviour in a quite magical way. But of course it is also fraught with paradoxes, and grey areas, once you start to think about it. For example; some people – doctors, charity workers, soldiers - deliberately put themselves in mortal danger as part of their idea of self-actualising, and this wouldn't make sense if the hierarchy were strictly sequential. Yet for all its faults, Maslow's hierarchy is a powerful explanatory and illustrative device: it gives us at least some means whereby we can understand our priorities as human beings trying to make our way through life.

And we can use Maslow's hierarchical schema to help us categorise the seemingly infinite forms of purposive crafting we humans engage in, and in doing so help us gain an insight into the whole process of modifying our lived environment. And we are able to do this because, as with human drives and needs, the multiplicity of phenomena on the surface can be usefully and meaningfully reduced to a mere handful of underlying principles.

So if we think in terms of very basic, very primitive, human needs – survival and safety needs – we can easily understand that we are really only talking about 'tools and weapons'. Tools for cooking and making shelters, and weapons for self-defence and hunting. There is not much more to primitive crafting than these elemental possibilities.

And having managed to establish a certain basic liveable environment, and a safe context in which to exist, other human needs and desires can start to present themselves. The desire to 'humanise' one's surroundings, closely followed by the desire to find ways to 'enjoy elements in life' over and above mere survival. The first involves design and decoration, and the second the ability to step back from the flow of everyday demands and 'reflect' – in various enjoyable and recreational ways – on the nature of lived experience itself. This sequential movement from the urgencies of survival to a more contemplative context is as true of the most technologically primitive societies as it is of the most advanced; we need first to secure a liveable environment and, having done so, we can start to think about how best to occupy our time. This is the self-evidently accurate process that Maslow identified in his hierarchy of needs.

So we start off by crafting for survival – making tools that will keep us alive – to crafting for the purposes of decorating and humanising the environment. And finally there is the question of recreation – in its widest sense, including both reflective activities and entertainment – and the question of 'spirituality' – attempts at taming and manipulating the combined forces of the imagination and the intellect.

We have always to bear in mind, of course, that none of the categories of either Maslow's hierarchy or the levels of crafting we have described ever fit into neat, non-paradoxical, easily identifiable boxes about which no more needs be said. Because each element in each schema can have multiple functions and multiple purposes and multiple dimensions to them all at one and the same time, and it's only by a process of abstraction that we are able to clarify, at any one moment, exactly 'what is what'. This might seem to imply that our whole discussion is arbitrary and subjective, and that we are simply making one possible case out of many, and that its opposite would be equally as true. But this is to lose sight of the bigger picture: just because there are grey areas at the edges does not mean that it does not make sense to follow what is, after all, a simple, straightforward and hardly-worth-denying conceptual trail as regards the most basic of human motivations, alongside the most basic types of crafted material. There are, for example, an infinite variety of foods on this planet, and an infinite variety of ways of preparing and presenting them, but it still makes sense to be able to identify, grasp and be able to apply a very general concept of 'food' in ordinary speech, despite the ever-present possibilities of paradox and uncertainty. This is all we are trying to do when following the conceptual trail regarding types of crafting, and the purposes to which the infinite variety of crafted material can be put.

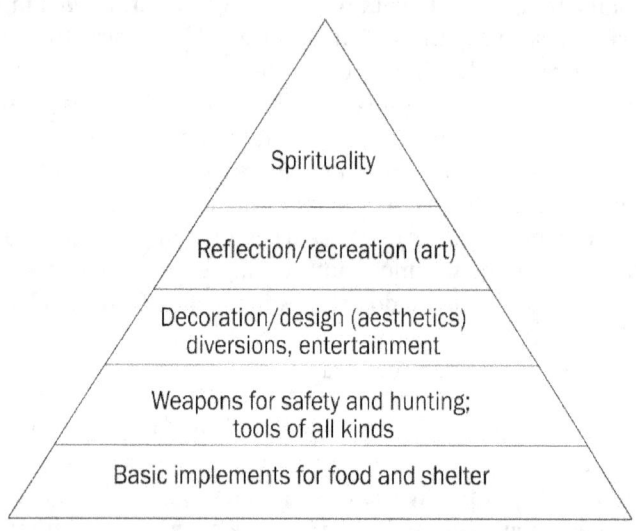

Hierarchy of crafting, based on Maslow

In the illustration above, we have applied the categories of crafted material to the types of human need as identified by Maslow. Crafting begins with simple toolmaking, and progresses from there to decoration and design, and ultimately to recreational presentations, and 'implements for spirituality'. In other words, from tools and weapons for survival, to books and buildings for spiritual purposes, and everything in between.

As has been said, these categories are only meant to be an approximation, and are more about gaining insight into the specific purposes behind the many varieties of crafting, than about classificatory precision. But this schema has the value of penetrating the mists that surround 'thinking about art' by identifying the key elements motivating, and giving meaning to, the various types of crafting human beings engage in. To be able to think in terms of simple motivations rather than trying to classify the seemingly unrelated varieties of crafted material is a massive step forward in 'getting to the point' of art, and understanding its essential characteristics. Modern art cannot be understood until a clear distinction is apparent between aesthetic crafting (centred on decorative attractiveness) and narrative art (centred on grasping experiential states of mind).

By combining the first two types of crafting (basic implements and weapons) we can further reduce the categories to three crucial and distinct requirements, namely <u>functional/utilitarian</u> (tools of every kind), <u>decorative</u> (anything crafted to make our environment look and feel more attractive) and <u>presentational</u> (material crafted for diversion, entertainment or reflection). Of course these categories overlap, and can combine purposes at one and the same time, but they usefully serve to distinguish between primary purposes. For example, a car is both a utilitarian machine and a decorative object, but its primary purpose as a mode of transport always 'outweighs' its value as a status symbol or aesthetic entity, except in extraordinary circumstances. Yes it would be possible to buy an expensive car solely to impress others, and never drive it, but then we are not really talking about a 'car' as a mode of transport as much as an item of jewellery, and the concept of a car – as normally understood – no longer applies. We can reverse the analogy and imagine an item of jewellery – normally a decorative aesthetic object only – being put to use to level off and stabilise a wobbly table; this does not suddenly call into question the categories we've outlined, it simply means that the jewellery is being treated as a mere stabilising lump of matter, and no longer as jewellery.

And as regards the category of 'spirituality' – as a realm we can meaningfully 'craft for' – we will deal in detail with this in a later section. The only point to be made at this stage – and one worth repeating regularly – is that as we move up the conceptual ladder, from gross crafting to more ethereal and conceptually based forms, most commentators feel free to indulge in conceptual mysticism, where everything is judged to be 'subjective', and no one feels entitled to tell the difference between one type of crafting and another, and 'all art is art' if you want it to be. Strident predilections are then the order of the day. But if we keep everything as simple and straightforward as possible, relating each type of crafting to its most basic elements, including its meaning and purpose, we will be able to reveal a valuable measure of objectivity that most art lovers are apparently unaware of. This has nothing to do with one's 'likes and dislikes', which are a separate issue.

Checklist of the basic forms of 'crafting', showing where 'art' can best be situated:

(1) Functional [utilitarian]:

tools / machinery / equipment /aids and assists

[can include the idea of '**design**': that is, modifications to crafted material to make it both ergonomic and attractive to handle, or to look at]

Examples: all forms of tools, machinery, gadgets, computers, educational aids, books, communication aids, etc.

(2) Decorative:

making the human lived environment – in its totality – look and feel attractive. Not to be confused with functional material, which is primarily utilitarian.

Examples: decorative architectural features, landscaped gardens, paintings in office foyers, objets d'art in houses, etc.

(3) Presentational [enjoyment, entertainment]:

material crafted for presentation – for the purposes of entertainment – to a targeted audience. Media [forms] include music, painting, sculpture, dance, theatre, film, fiction, video, performance etc. Also included in this category are sports and games.

Within which there are three subcategories:

(a) ordinary presentational craft:

This covers crafted material which either fails in its intention to achieve either **(b)** or **(c)**, or did not aspire to them in the first place, but which is nevertheless intended to be presentational, diverting and entertaining

Examples: mainstream films, plays, novels, sports, games, etc.

(b) aesthetic craft:

presentational objects crafted primarily for the sensorial delight afforded by the chosen medium itself, hopefully manifesting qualities of beauty and splendour

Examples: Cezanne, Matisse, Jackson Pollock, Brancusi, Brahms, etc.

(c) art:

presentational media which deliberately or inadvertently reveals the 'strange and disturbing' – the unsettling, the provoking, the uncanny, the fascinating

Examples: Francis Bacon, David Lynch, Andy Warhol, Joseph Beuys, etc.

NB: all three categories –
functional, decorative and presentational
– can and do overlap to varying degrees, depending on the context. But it is their **primary purpose** as crafted material which distinguishes one specific type from another.

(4) Spirituality

The use of crafted material as part of a quest for meaning, spiritual knowledge and understanding, and fulfilment as a human being. This category ranges from the most primitive to the most ethereal, and includes all varieties of magic, mysticism and religion, as well as everything commonly understood to be psychological.

Examples: certain books, drugs, buildings, clothing, states of mind, rituals, etc

Discussion: the conceptual issues

The most difficult distinction to clarify with any finality at this stage is that between decorative and aesthetic crafting, mainly because they are forms of one another, and really only exist as endpoints on a sliding scale. In other words, given very slight changes of perspective, they are almost interchangeable. If I arrange a few pencils in a box according to colour, I'm engaging in a certain minimal aesthetic practice, and the whole sorting procedure doesn't really rise to the level of 'a work' – as in an 'artwork' – so I'm really just achieving a low level of 'decoration' or beautification. But if my pencil sorting involved thousands of pencils laid out on a table – even if they were put to actual use – the display might rise to the level of an aesthetic event, and become something of an aesthetic object, appreciable in its own right. It's all a matter of degree, and context, and the perspective rests on a series of implicit assumptions which can appear and disappear depending on the moment.

> **Illustration: Alexander Calder sculpture, for example the red 'Flamingo' (1973) in Federal Plaza, Chicago, Illinois.**

This does not mean that we can't differentiate between the many layers appearing in close proximity to one another, or identify the moment they change from being one thing and become another. For example, imagine a bare, windswept concrete forecourt fronting a newly constructed office building. Someone in authority decides to buy a 'work of art' to display in a prominent position, and so spends many millions on a brightly coloured Alexander Calder sculpture. The Calder is both an aesthetic object – to be admired for its sensual qualities – as well as a visually decorative item, designed to humanise by the introduction of a splash of colour what might otherwise be a desolate forecourt. Those seeking it out deliberately as 'a work by Calder' would view it in a certain light, but those walking past it every day would soon relegate it, through familiarity, to the background, and to them its decorative qualities – the colour against the concrete, if they even notice it at all after a month or two – would be its key feature.

Now the person behind the purchase and positioning of the Calder sculpture may well have had some other ideas in addition to his or her idea of aesthetics – a political statement, perhaps, or an expression of a wider philosophy of life – but short of expressing them in some public way, there is no way we could know, just from looking at the sculpture itself, what they were. But it is important to recognise that these additional philosophical, political or spiritual ideas are not, strictly speaking, integral to the aesthetics of the object, even if people want them to be, because this would be to confuse the boundaries between one aspect of an object with another, and if allowed to persist will result in a collapse of any possible clarity of thought.

Example: impressionism vs socialist realism

If we are to understand 'art' clearly and decisively, we need to be able to discriminate meaningfully between the different layers present in visual phenomena. For example, an impressionist painting of flowers, and a Stalinist poster exhorting workers to greater efforts do not, even as visual objects with aesthetic dimensions, ever amount to 'the same thing': they may both at base be 'things you look at', but they have quite different meanings and purposes. The flower painting is a purely aesthetic object; the Stalinist poster is a political directive; in the flower painting the aesthetics are meant to be enjoyed for their own sake, as an end in themselves; in the Stalinist poster the aesthetics have been deployed for socio-political purposes, and have therefore become a mere device, or a ploy.

> **Illustrations: examples of 'Socialist realism' in art, as appeared in the Soviet Union, Maoist China and Communist Eastern Europe.**

It is of course perfectly possible to ignore the socio-political dimension of socialist realist crafting and focus instead on the aesthetics, and in so doing treating the posters and paintings not as examples of sugar coated edicts, but simply as colours and shapes and slogans. The pictures and letterings are then judged wholly in terms of their visual attractiveness, with all other considerations secondary. There is nothing inherently illegitimate about re-contextualising an object, and giving it a new interpretation - examples of which are widespread across the arts – but it does run the risk of perpetuating the very real confusions that muddy popular conceptions about 'art'. It encourages the limiting idea that there is nothing to be gained by carefully distinguishing between the different perspectives required to assess crafted material on its own terms, and that you can meaningfully lump everything into one category, and approach all 'art' as a matter of visual candy.

The importance of understanding the concept of the contextualisation of art will be dealt with in more detail in a later section. Suffice to say right now that the ability to differentiate between the many possible perspectives one can adopt in viewing and assessing a crafted object is crucial to an understanding of the difference between 'aesthetics' and 'art proper', and is therefore crucial to an appreciation of what we will go on to define as 'art' itself, as a distinct and substantial entity in its own right, quite separate from the realms of beauty and truth and sensorial aesthetics.

Summary: the main forms of crafted material

What we have tried to explain in this section is the way it is possible to gain insight into the various types of crafting we human beings interact with, by framing it in terms of a hierarchy of wants and needs, inspired in part by Maslow's schema. The tools and implements we use are a direct expression of desires and needs we want fulfilled, and we can gain a very useful and illuminating insight into what we label as 'art' by approaching it from the point of view of what we are trying 'to do' with that particular form of crafting. When it comes down to it, our most crucial human needs are relatively few in number – even if manifold in expression and actualisation – and by focussing on these principles we can dispel the persistent fog of 'art mysticism'.

5

THE CONCEPTUAL TRAIL FROM "AESTHETIC CRAFT" TO "ART"

The distinction we want to draw in this chapter is that between 'aesthetics' – crafting to achieve presentational beauty and sensorial delight – and 'art' – meaning crafting to achieve some sort of 'presentational narrative'. Aesthetics is all about skilled technique in the service of manifestly beautiful crafting; art is about the presentation of narrative. Classical craftworks of the sort one encounters in museums and national galleries are examples of aesthetics; modern artworks – wherever one might encounter them – and to the extent that they embody the principles of 'art' as defined here, are narrative objects which cannot be understood unless one can discern the narrative possibilities underpinning them. Art always involves picking up on the perspective embodied in the artwork.

This does not mean that every modern artwork manages to convey something like a 'worthwhile' or 'substantial' narrative: in fact most attempts at modern art are derivative and feeble, and have no story to tell at all. Many modern artists, not being either fully confident or even fully cognisant of their mission, often include features of classicism in what they do, in the hope that if they fail to make a 'modern' statement they might at least be admired for their technical skills. But real art can convey real substance and real meaning without the least trace of classical form or academic training.

In the previous chapter we discussed the various types of purposeful crafting we human beings engage in, and what these various types of craft – reduced to their bare elements – are expressions of. And we saw that, in line with a Maslowian hierarchy of needs, the various types of crafting can meaningfully and illuminatingly be reduced to

    (a) the production of utilitarian implements,

    (b) decorations,

    (c) diversional and recreational objects, and

    (d) assists for spirituality.

There is really not much else of importance out there – in terms of crafting - if anything at all. Every implement one can think of will fit into one or other basic category, and often into more than one; but if we stick to the concept of 'primary purpose' when assigning an object to a category, we will not become confused as to what an object has been created and crafted for. This does not mean that we are unable to appreciate secondary and tertiary levels of meaning and purpose, but rather that we avoid lapsing into the kind of mystical confusion that characterises popular thought about art, where politics and spirituality and environmentalism are all mixed into a mystifying fog, and nobody really knows what's going on, and art is left to become 'whatever you want it to be'. With a bit of effort, it is possible to discriminate between different levels of meaning, and assign seemingly diverse phenomena to very specific and distinct categories without distorting or disregarding their elemental qualities. It is then possible to define 'art' in an illuminating and practicable way.

The decorative aspect to crafting

The desire to decorate both the human body and all objects in the lived environment is widespread in all societies, and can be taken as a given. From the point of view of our discussion, the important aspect of decorative crafting that we need to highlight is that moment in our 'looking at an object' when we change our perspective from thinking how we are going to use it, to simply enjoying - or not enjoying - the look of it, as an activity in itself. We have the ability to switch from treating an object as a tool, or an implement, to enjoying it for its sensorial characteristics alone, without any thought as to using them for some further instrumental purpose. A common grey kettle, for example, can pass unnoticed in a family kitchen for years, but if it gets replaced by a bright yellow enamel one, it might, in the eyes of some, and for a time at least, become an object of wonder; and not for its functional usability, but rather for its startling 'look'. The kettle gets admired for its appearance, and these moments of admiration are something of an end in themselves – we don't think of them as necessary gateways to some further lines of thought. And this idea of admiring something for its sensorial qualities alone is of course the basis of what can be termed the 'aesthetic gaze', and by extension 'aesthetics' itself.

Aesthetic crafting and 'design'

We know from cultural artefacts – Viking daggers, Eskimo spears, Greek vases, and so on – that decorating useful items to make them look attractive goes back to the earliest times in human history. As was said before, we can't be sure right now that decoration served exactly the same aesthetic purpose that it would today, but intuition tells us that at least some moments in the act of admiring the finished product must have involved aesthetic pleasure for its own sake. There are many sections in the early chapters of the Christian Old Testament which speak about the aesthetics of sacrifices and offerings as 'pleasing to the Lord' when we know that what is really meant is 'pleasing to those performing them'; but even in such circumstances there is still a difference between supposedly pleasing the Lord, and merely pleasing yourself. Generally speaking, we don't visit art galleries and museums with the idea of pleasing someone other than ourselves, or with motives other than admiring the objects on display for the interest they can afford us.

But we also need to distinguish between the aesthetics of an object – those features which are attractive to our senses – and the utilitarian concept of crafted 'design', even though many objects are now 'aesthetically designed', meaning deliberately designed to look good, irrespective of how well or badly they function. 'Design' in a utilitarian and ergonomic sense is about finding ways to craft an object so that it is maximally efficient, and does whatever it is supposed to do with great precision and ease of application. This is especially the case with machinery and engines which, at least in the early stages of their evolution, are strictly means to achieving specific ends, and it is only after these ends have been reached that someone would start to think in terms of machine aesthetics and user-friendliness.

All this is simply to say that although aesthetics and design are very much linked in practice, we can distinguish between the aesthetic gaze – enjoying the sensations for their own sake – and thinking about an object in terms of its useful functionality, whatever form that functionality may take. What we are working towards here is the ability to discriminate between the various crucially different perspectives we bring to an object, as a prelude to a full appreciation of the dimensions of the concept of 'presentation', in which an object is ultimately contemplated and enjoyed for the kind of narrative it embodies, above and beyond any aesthetic value it may have. This is not as complicated as it may sound, as many familiar objects contain 'narratives' of the type we are referring to here.

The concept of 'presentation'

The 'aesthetic gaze' is the first step on the road to the idea of objects and crafted works as 'items of presentation'. When we gaze at something aesthetically, we are, as it were, standing back and admiring the features of the crafted object as sensorial experiences alone – at least to begin with. Our experience of the sensations may then awaken all kinds of other thoughts in us, but these secondary thoughts are always grounded – based – on the range of sensual excitations we experience when we encounter the object, either directly, or through a medium, such as an illustration or a recording. We encounter some artworks visually; some aurally; and insofar as these crafted objects are principally or entirely aesthetic – meaning primarily intended to be objects of sensorial beauty – our experience of the object is meant to be aesthetic, not imaginative, or spiritual, or psychological, or anything else. This does not mean that aesthetic experiences are grossly and bluntly physical, simply limited to a cloud of sensual immediacy, but we have to be careful to distinguish between unrestrained flights of the imagination, and what we can meaningfully say is our experience of the crafted object in front of us.

Da Vinci's 'Mona Lisa', and its experiential parameters

For example, Da Vinci's Mona Lisa, if we restrict ourselves to describing it in simplistic narrative terms, is the portrait of a mysteriously self-contained and enigmatic figure whose life and thoughts we can only guess at, and who represents a window onto a distant and remote world. The landscape backdrop is improbable and somewhat sinister, almost a scene from another planet, but we mostly disregard it as an irrelevance. And despite the prevailing mood of a somewhat stultifying serenity, the painting also contains an underlying tension in that it encourages us to stare expectantly at her expression in the hope that it might suddenly reveal itself, even though we know that this isn't going to happen.

And all the while, we cannot but be aware of Da Vinci's extraordinary achievement, both in terms of his technical skill, and the magnificence of the outcome. Anyone who has ever tried to draw anything, let alone dabble with paint, will know that classical skill of this kind is almost otherworldly, and a source of constant wonder. It boils down to the simple question, 'How on earth do you do that ?', and even when you know the answer is 'combine huge talent with painstakingly gained technical skill', the whole thing seems unsettlingly magical.

What else can we say about the simple sight – the simple visual image – of the Mona Lisa which is not, in some way, already covered here ? We can discuss her clothing, her hairstyle, her posture, and so on, and of course in doing so we add intellectual layers to our experience of the painting which, insofar as we remember them when we next see it, will in a very ordinary and everyday way colour our experience of what we see. And there are all kinds of other interpretative narratives waiting in the wings, some of them salacious and intriguing, but what have they got to do with the painting itself ? The fact is, not very much, and to the extent that we rely on them for our enjoyment of it, we wholly miss the point of the aesthetic experience itself. In other words, there are boundaries – parameters – to the immediacy and directness of the central aesthetic experience of a presentational object, and if we venture beyond them, we need to understand that we are replacing one kind of experience with something quite different.

> Illustration: Leonardo's Mona Lisa (c. 1503-1517): high definition versions can be found online, as can scholarly documentaries on YouTube.

This doesn't mean that a freewheeling interpretation of an artwork, going off in all directions, and ending up talking about something quite other, is somehow illegal or not permitted: no one is going to stop you, nor should they. But if we want to be clear about the limits of a certain type of interpretation, and the beginnings of another very different type, we need to be able to distinguish clearly between the aesthetic experience of the object we have in front of us, and that of losing ourselves in semi-mystical reverie. The Mona Lisa is the Mona Lisa; it's not about a prostitute whose lover murdered an Italian royal; or about a woman suffering from some undiagnosed physical or mental illness, or about some emptyheaded teenager earning some pocket money as a model. It's about the direct effect on us of the image we see directly in front of us – this face, this expression, this pose, this background – all combining to create its own unique magic and mystery and, as is the case with any single static image, its own inevitable limitations. Mona Lisa's world doesn't really speak to us with any great urgency or compulsion, and there is something faintly tedious about the whole painting which the astonishing technical magic of the eyes and the smile cannot quite dispel. It's not the most interesting thing one can think of to look at for any length of time.

Where does this leave us, as viewers ? Simply to say that the Mona Lisa is a very clear instance of an 'aesthetic object', and that as soon as we start pursuing other thoughts that the painting might awaken in us - beyond its sensorial and crafterly qualities - we depart from the Mona Lisa as a painting – and as an experiential image - and begin to move into a different experiential realm altogether. Non-aesthetic thoughts inspired by an aesthetic object are not properly part of its essential purpose.

Interim summary: utilitarian objects, presentational objects, and aesthetics

Central to any modern conception of art – whether the prevailing popular conception or the more specialised one we are arguing for here – is the idea of being able to present an object to an audience in the understanding that the object be admired and appreciated for its manifest qualities alone, and not for any functional use to which it might be put. Put differently, 'art' is about a certain way of 'looking at things', a certain very specific 'gaze', with which we are all very familiar, even if we haven't thought much about it, and so haven't grasped it with any clarity. And this 'gaze' is one we adopt when we stand back and assess something in terms of the impact of its sensual – sensorial – features on us, and we enjoy the sensual impact as an end in itself, with no thought of putting our reactions to some other use. We enjoy what we see, or hear, or feel, just for the enjoyment of the enjoyment itself, no more, no less. The rationale and logic of this enjoyment of presentational enjoyment – such as it is – is the logic of 'aesthetics'. 'Aesthetics' is all about understanding the way in which presentational objects work their sensorial magic on us.

All of us are very familiar with the idea of presentational objects when it comes to popular music, in that pop musicians present us with items of music – using various media - to be enjoyed for their own sake. Music can additionally be used for social or political or mystical ends, but these are secondary to its direct sensual impact on us, and it is important for an understanding of art to be able to distinguish the primary from the secondary; that is, the impact of the aesthetic features from interpretative layers which are not aesthetic in nature.

And the concept of 'presentational' needs to be extended to represent all those crafted works whose primary context involves us, as the audience, 'standing back' to admire the sensorial features we are being presented with. This includes every conceivable artform, from the most minimal sculptural object, like a rock in a garden, to the most cerebral crafting of ideas, as might be encountered in a poem or work of literature. 'Presentation' involves an interplay between creator, their creation, and at least the concept of an audience – even if it can't always be found ! – and although this is an unstable and dynamic relationship, it is quite different in its essential nature from the relationship that exists between say, a toolmaker, the tools that they fashion, and the person who puts those implements to use.

As we will go on to explain, the idea of a 'presentational object' is only the beginning of the conceptual trail leading from 'craft' to 'art'. We begin with tools and implements, and we end up with items crafted to be enjoyed as objects of enjoyment in themselves. The most basic of these types of crafted objects are aesthetic works; items whose raison d'etre is the representation of beauty and beautiful technique.

The realm beyond aesthetics, namely 'art'

Understanding the difference between tools-for-use and presentational objects is relatively straightforward, but the difference between aesthetic objects and art objects – as subsets of presentational objects – is more complicated. This is because art objects are frequently confused for aesthetic objects, even by the professionals who have dedicated their lives to increasing our understanding of the subject. The confusion is justifiable in the sense that art and aesthetic objects can fulfil both functions at one and the same time, and both are quintessentially presentational, and seem - if you are not alert to the many very different layers of meaning - to be all of a piece. And in order to pick our way carefully through this confusion and misdirection, we will need to return to analysing the layers of the popular perception of art, in order to see why this view is so pervasive and why, in the long run, it is likely to remain the default option for most people.

6

"ART MYSTICISM", BOHEMIANISM, AND CREATIVITY

Problems with vocabulary

In this chapter we are going to identify those aspects of popular, everyday 'thought about art' which contribute most to the ongoing mystification and misdirection preventing clarification as to what art might be 'in itself'. And one of the problems we run into right at the outset concerns that of a lack of helpful vocabulary, especially when it comes to labelling the different perspectives people adopt when they immerse themselves, mentally, into what they think of as 'art'. This is to be expected, given that our ordinary, everyday 'frames of mind' are hard to identify and characterise at the best of times. Vocabulary depends for its usefulness on its ability to help us label – accurately - a range of hazy and potentially confusing phenomena, such that we are then able to think clearly and confidently about them; but when it comes to the experience of 'art', people like to abandon their ability to differentiate and discriminate on the basis of ideas, and simply to give way to their own sensual prejudices and predilections relating to whatever it is that has been presented to them, and then to have those unmediated responses – in effect, their 'feelings and sensations' – act as the justification for their thoughts and opinions. Indeed, half the attraction of 'artiness' and the 'arty' frame of mind is its celebration of a kind of subjective, self-validating sensual enjoyment, where intellect and clarity of thought are always subservient to passion and sentiment and simple aesthetic prejudice.

And even here, where we use terms like 'passion' and 'sentiment', these words don't really accurately illuminate the states of mind in question, and are just blunt approximations for a whole range of possibilities. However, even if we are unable to find existing technical terms for each key aesthetic response, we can at least describe these phenomena in detail such that they are clearly identified and differentiated one from another.

Bohemianism, and creativity

We are going to begin by examining the idea that the artistic mindset is to be located somewhere within a potent brew of bohemianism, and creativity. This will not of itself show us where art is, but it will show us where many people *think* it is, and it will also show us why the whole notion of 'art' is shrouded in a cloud of mystification.

Artists are always associated, in the popular imagination, with an openness to creativity, and a predisposition toward a bohemian lifestyle. Each is believed to be closely related to the other: you can't be creative if your lifestyle won't let you respond to it; and you encourage creativity by letting it dictate how you live. In totalitarian regimes, creative people are forced to conform, and are often restricted to exercising their crafting skills in the very narrow service of the state, and this tends to be viewed by the rest of us as a form of privation and disempowerment, underlining our belief in artists as people who should somehow be exempt from routines associated with a 'nine-to-five' work schedule.

And also in the popular view, bohemian lifestyles tend to be characterised by the liberal use of drugs and alcohol, and by sexual promiscuity, unconventional dress codes, idiosyncratic diets, and erratic bedtimes. As one might expect, irresponsibility and selfishness often seep into the mix, as does mental illness. This is not to judge 'bohemianism' – it sounds like fun, after all - but simply to identify some of its possible downsides. And the point is that, rightly or wrongly, most 'artists' – we have yet to define this vocation with any precision – believe that an unstructured, libertarian lifestyle offers them the optimal context within which to do whatever it is they want to do.

'Creativity', as a propensity, or as a characteristic some people may be said to possess, is more difficult to define. For our purposes it is enough to say that a creative person is one who, given a task, is able to come up with new and imaginative solutions to it; and if we situate this ability in an artistic context, we would say that a creative artist is one who is able to realise original ideas, over and above the exercise of learned skills and techniques.

But from our point of view the most important characteristic underlying the idea of the 'creative bohemian' is that it locates the whole artistic enterprise in a kind of region of irrationality and deliberate disorder, where an extreme openness to the impulses of creativity means that spontaneity and an unrestrained responsiveness take precedence over carefully controlled logical analyses. 'Existential disorder' is, as it were, the price one has to pay for the privilege of originality. And in a way, as part of the enjoyable colour of life, we can say that society expects and encourages its artistic community to misbehave, not only for entertaining headlines and scandals, but as a consequence of this much deeper belief in the idea of a binding contract between creativity and irrationality.

Modern life and its features: pursuing meaning and fulfilment

Now to the extent that we understand the way 'art' is integrated into modern life, and where it is 'situated' relative to other pursuits, we will also understand something of the way human beings attempt to find meaningful conditions and circumstances for themselves, as a way of giving their lives some sense of purpose and coherence.

So far we are still referring to 'art' as if we know what it is, yet without having defined it in any substantial way. This is unavoidable until we have sorted through the various layers of mystification that art encourages as part of its appeal. At this stage we are only concerned to identify and describe the most important aspects of 'art mystification' insofar as they relate to the way people make use of their idea of art as part of a quest for meaning and fulfilment in life.

Most of us are introduced to art at school, where we learn that art is a form of creative play; and this play quickly comes to be contrasted with the more demanding scholarship required to master other subjects. A select few begin to display obvious talent – which at an early age is usually a matter of skill in drawing – and they might find themselves, over the years, thinking in terms of 'art' as a career choice. Yet by the time any such decision needs to be made, we will all have absorbed the idea that those who choose to be artists will do so because they have recognised it as a pursuit that best answers their very specific needs: being an artist is not, generally speaking, something you would end up doing by mistake, or by accident. Art – meaning a specific type of creative and visionary crafting – is, therefore, from this point of view, very much 'a calling', a vocation.

There is of course also the world of commercial art and design, and although this is a specialised field requiring particular talents, it is much less of a calling than visionary art, because it is so closely dependent on market forces and business practices. Commercial art is tailored to fashion and trends and budgets, and success is measured in terms of money-making, not in terms of the realisation of a particular artistic vision.

And having absorbed through schooling a vague but functionally practicable conception of what 'art' is, and what art can do, most people enter adulthood with an idea of art as enjoyable in its own way, but peripheral to the demands of everyday life. We are all aware – at least subliminally – of the ubiquity of popular art in the way it decorates and enhances the look and feel of existence itself – pop songs, billboards, neon, fashion – but we probably don't appreciate how drab and monotonous life would be without it, just as we don't appreciate the extent to which the interplay of images we encounter through various media contributes to our ordinary sense of positivity and human connectedness.

Yet even though popular art plays a crucial and perhaps even a determining role in everyday life - affecting our moods and dispositions in important ways - this doesn't allow us to alter the fact that this decorative, contextual element to existence is largely peripheral to our centre of attention. In other words, we might miss it when it's gone, but most of the time we are not really aware of it, and take it as a given. This is true of many key features of everyday life: we only become aware of their importance when they go wrong, in the same way that, having satisfied certain basic bodily needs in our hierarchy, we can move on up the scale, able to turn our attention elsewhere.

However, the decorative, contextual element to popular art is not the end of the story. There is a point at which people turn to presentational material for more than mere pleasurable everyday reassurance, when they start to search for meaning and purpose. But the world of presentational crafting is, as we have seen, shot through with mystification and confusion, and this makes it difficult for us to negotiate other than in an amateurish and haphazard fashion.

The endorsement of 'high culture' by religion

The search for meaning in life usually takes people, sooner or later, to religion; and religion in this context involves, in addition to a philosophy of life, a sense of belonging, as well as a sense of how best to live from day to day, what to do in life, and how to go about doing it. Religion, whether a New Age cult or an orthodox teaching, offers a complete package, and a complete system of belief and practice which, theoretically at least, can be said to cover every eventuality.

But in our sceptical, scientifically-oriented societies, religious doctrines have, to a certain extent, felt the need to adapt to the changing conditions. Whereas in pre-modern times societies might have felt that artforms – from painting to music to literature – were, with a few exceptions, vaguely sinful and worldly, modern religious doctrines have found ways to endorse what they perceive to be high culture – so-called 'serious' music, serious painting, serious film-making, and so on; serious being essentially equivalent to 'deeply conservative' – and perhaps tolerating small doses of low culture – pop music, dancing, sport, entertainments – provided no one is in any doubt as to the superiority of the so-called high culture over the low.

This has led to a symbiotic relationship between the ideas of 'high culture' and that of 'spiritual worthiness', in the sense that exposure to the so-called 'great works of art' is considered spiritually beneficial, and an all-round good thing both for the individual and for society. The precise dynamics of this relationship, historical and contemporary, is too vast and complex a subject to do more than mention in passing here, other than to say that it plays an important role in validating the role of culture in society, and contributing to its long term maintenance.

The secular quest for meaning through the arts: from the casual gallery-goer to the cultural gourmand

But although the churches play a significant role in supporting culture, financially and morally, the secularisation of society has generated its own secular quests for meaning and purpose, and it is these forces which are unquestionably the primary agents for the idea that artforms need to be taken seriously, and that they are a potential source of psychological and quasi-mystical redemption. When religious doctrines lose their power to persuade, we find ourselves drifting towards those alternatives which offer an avenue for self-improvement and self-development, coupled with at least the distant promise of a form of rapture, however fleeting. Music is the most accessible and easily understood example, but for those with different sensibilities, any of the other artforms would be just as good.

We are not saying that 'music', for example, can, as such, act as an adequate substitute for religion; or even that there are people who might think it could. But as a supposedly virtuous cultural option – at least in its classical guise – it seems to many people to point in the direction of sensitising oneself towards something 'higher' and something 'more noble', and in this sense contributes towards making life seem more meaningful. There can also be 'lifestyles' centred on music which go some way to offering people a philosophy of life in both theory and practice: these lifestyles would range from being a full-time musician, to someone who regularly goes to concerts and who listens closely and conscientiously to recordings, almost as acts of secular communion. The music itself offers an immersive, quasi-mystical experience of its own, but the crucial idea underlying the whole engagement is the belief that participation in a particular artform is somehow salutary, and improving, and good for the soul. People like to believe that their refined sensitivities make them better people, and they use their engagement with a chosen artform as a way of imbuing their lives with a sense of worthiness, and perhaps even a touch of nobility.

The quest for meaning through the arts then creates an inevitable continuum stretching from the casual gallery-goer, to the Sunday painter, to the dedicated cultural gourmand. These are people who make a deliberate decision to engage with the arts in some way, believing – also in 'some way' – that this engagement is to their benefit, in terms of a mysterious connection to 'realms of meaning' above and beyond the merely functional, and the merely utilitarian. There is enjoyment to be had in the direct engagement with the artwork itself, but this enjoyment feels connected to a more expansive cosmic sense of meaning and purpose.

The idea of engaging with culture as essentially 'worthy'

Another important dimension to the idea of art as a source of meaning, is the complex idea of 'cultural worthiness', wherein we engage with artforms not because we find them enjoyable, but because in doing so we believe we uphold values that are worth upholding. This is closely tied in with the idea of the endorsement of high culture by religion and other conservative forces, in the name of some mysterious, quasi-spiritual, 'greater cultural good'.

'Worthiness' – in the terms we are discussing here – is one of those conceptions that exist on the periphery of popular consciousness, never quite coming into view, and seldom analysed head on; yet its power to motivate should not be underestimated. We are referring here in particular to the idea of 'worthiness by association', and 'worthiness by associative osmosis', as opposed to the idea of 'worthiness by virtuous engagement', in which one makes a deliberate decision to improve one's cultural sensitivities by some kind of practice or study. 'Worthiness by association' involves doing something because you think it's 'good for you' in some morally virtuous, quasi-spiritual way, rather than because you actually want to do it. Finding yourself attending a Shakespeare play, or going to a Monet exhibition, or to a Mozart opera, and telling yourself how 'wonderful' the experience is, might be examples; these are standard cultural events in western society, and the tens of thousands who flock to them can't all be enthusiasts and aficionados; it would be surprising if more than a handful are.

'Worthiness' can't be equated with mere hypocrisy and self-deception, because we can genuinely come to like things which at the outset we only pretend to like; and the very process of education itself – whatever the subject – always involves starting at a point where our likes and dislikes are irrelevant, and we simply have to adapt to the required circumstances. What we are trying to point out is that, despite our earlier characterisation of 'art' as the realm of the hedonistic, self-indulgent 'creative bohemian', there is another equally important element to the maintenance of cultural norms, high and low; and this is the received idea of culture as essentially 'worthy' in some quasi-spiritual way, over and above our likes and dislikes. Even the most creative of bohemians spend at least a part of their lives pretending to like things they don't, in the hope that it will benefit them at some future moment.

So if we were to strip away the element of 'enjoyability' from culture – in other words, the idea that culture is maintained by people who genuinely enjoy engaging with it in its many forms – we would still be left with the realm of 'worthiness', whereby culture is maintained, and passed on from generation to generation, by a resilient conservatism, consisting of a belief that this is what we 'ought to do', even in the absence of it affording us any pleasure in the process. This is how 'canons' – collections of supposedly the best examples of a particular artform – of one sort or another come to be assembled, and how these canons act as the necessary yardstick against which everything else is set, and against which everything is judged, for better or worse.

Section summary: the array of forces contributing to 'art mysticism'

Earlier we contrasted the difference between viewing an object in terms of its functional usefulness, with viewing it presentationally, in terms of its aesthetic and narrative qualities. The connection between functional usefulness and everyday life is relatively straightforward, but the connection between viewing something presentationally and its meaningfulness in everyday life is much more problematic, and very rapidly descends into confusion and, as we describe it here, a type of 'mysticism'.

What do we mean by this 'mysticism' ? We mean that when people switch from utilitarian to presentational perspectives, they then have no clear guiding principles as to how best to proceed, so simply resort to ideas they have picked up along the way, some ideas coming from their education, and some from what they have heard and read. 'Art' is experienced as an open-ended 'free-for-all', with one's likes and dislikes as the deciding factor; but this 'arty' state of mind is more than an exercise in instant prejudice, it is very much an altered state of consciousness, with possibilities stretching from ephemeral perceptions to trancelike reveries.

And fuelling this aesthetic altered state is the belief that those feelings and sensations and thoughts that artworks arouse in me - the viewer - which justify themselves in the absence of anyone to tell me otherwise, are, in the last resort, what 'art' is all about; so 'art' then becomes a matter of my 'arty mystical states' or 'experiences'. And this is reinforced by the fact that the creative bohemians who create art are always up to all kinds of extraordinary things, creatively and behaviourally, so there is no reason for me to think that art is anything other than my free-flowing 'arty state of mind'.

'Art mysticism' also applies just as much to those who, subscribing to a deeply conservative perspective on aesthetics, believe their responses to classical artworks to be highly refined, and sophisticated, and elegant. It is not the degree of abandonment to sensation which is important here, as much as the fact that art is widely believed to be all about giving yourself over to the altered state of 'artiness'. So we end up in a situation where 'art' is widely understood to be located in a realm of self-validating 'feelings' and 'sensations' and 'states of mind', and there appears to be nothing in popular thought about art which in any way goes against this, even if we include intellectual art criticism in the mix.

But more than anything else, art mysticism persists because the principles of art – that is to say, the key ideas which hold art together – have yet to be clearly elucidated, and widely accepted. As things stand, 'art', and our experience of it, is something of a superficial affair, with no intellectual underpinning to speak of: everyone likes to rely on their own personal ideas of taste and aesthetic perception as authoritative.

7

SO THEN, WHAT EXACTLY IS "ART"?

    To understand 'art', as opposed to 'aesthetic craft', we have to clarify the distinction between presentational works designed to appeal to our senses – mainly the senses of sight, touch, and hearing – and works which appeal to our narrative imagination. Presentational works which appeal to our senses – paintings, sculptures, pieces of music, ballet and so on – are examples of 'aesthetic craft', and they are generally intended to appeal to our sense of beauty, and sensorial (sensual) magnificence, and attractiveness. And insofar as they arouse some sense of beauty in us, they have achieved their purpose, and can be considered, for what it is worth, 'good' – meaning 'good art', or better, 'good craft' – in other words, 'good' at what it is they do.

    'Art', on the other hand, goes beyond aesthetic sensation, and is intended to appeal to our imaginative faculties. Artworks are meant to be portals to realms of the imagination, whether by narrative, or by perspectival-altering means; artworks invite you to take on a perspective, and then to inhabit it, and to experience it from within. With an object of aesthetic craft, what you see, or what you hear, is more or less exactly 'what you get'; with an art object, what you see or what you hear is only the beginning – the entry point – to an imaginative experience of sorts, which involves the viewer being directed by the artwork into a specific experiential realm. And to the extent that an artwork is able to direct the viewer into a specific imaginative realm, then it would count as 'good art'. 'Taking on a perspective and inhabiting it' is not as complicated as it may sound, and is a very straightforward, familiar and everyday experience which we are all capable of as part of a basic psychological human capacity. This ability that we have to enter into 'other mindsets' will be explored in detail in a later section.

The 'Mona Lisa' is an example of aesthetic craft; it is all about appreciating the sublime technique on display, as well as the magnificence of the enigmatic image of the girl herself. It could also be seen as the starting point of a kind of imaginative reverie, perhaps along the lines of 'who is this girl, and what sort of world did she live in ?', but this type of rather obvious prompted questioning could be stimulated by more or less anything one comes across in daily life, and isn't specific to aesthetic presentational objects, nor is it their primary purpose: most classical aesthetic objects are meant to be enjoyed for their sensual qualities alone.

> **Illustration: see Joseph Beuys 'Fat Chair' (1964), though other examples of Beuys's use of fat as a sculptural medium will do just as well.**

An excellent example of an 'art object' – by our definition - would be something like Joseph Beuys's 'Fat Chair' (1964), which consists of a simple wooden chair, a triangular wedge of fat covering the seat, and what looks like a twisted length of wire sticking out of the fat; not exactly a conventionally beautiful object like Michelangelo's David. No sign of either classical beauty in the form, or studied skill in the construction, and so by traditional standards we would have to judge it an aesthetic disaster. Beuys's chair simply makes no sense as an object of classical – or modern – beauty, and for this reason many would deny it a place in art at all. But in terms of an entry point into the imaginative, perspectival experiences Beuys has created, it has its own unique power and ability to fascinate.

How does the 'Fat Chair' work ? Basically it is saying, 'Come into my world, and experience it on its own terms'; it is not asking to be compared, as a matter of technical execution, to the Mona Lisa. But how do you get into the Beuys world ? There are many ways of doing this, but the simplest would be to seek out more of his creations, and see if something like a distinctive experiential landscape – a mindset, in other words – begins to emerge; the more you know about Beuys, the more his peculiar artistic worldview, and mindset, starts to cohere, and the more his strange creations start to work their distinctive magic. This is not about having the Beuys world 'make sense' in everyday worldly terms, and interpreting his artworks as items of allegorical meaning, as if they were visual crossword puzzles; rather this is about artistic sense, where experiential creations can be completely illogical, irrational and impossible to translate, and can ultimately defy explanation of any kind. This is because good 'art' exists in its own distinctive realm, and does not have to conform to our everyday ways of thinking. 'Art' is about achieving 'mental congruence' – to use an ugly psychotherapeutic term – with the perspective underpinning, and giving meaning to, the artwork. If you can join Beuys in his imaginative autobiographical art world, then his artworks will start to reveal themselves.

'Art' as an 'overall effect', not as individual standalone aesthetic objects

We can illustrate this in everyday terms by examining the very familiar idea of stylish home decorating. Imagine visiting a home that has been carefully decorated in a specific way, with the owner striving to achieve an overall atmospheric 'effect' of some kind. The key to grasping the look and feel of the house is located in the overall 'effect', not in the various individual items which may have been deployed to achieve it. Of course the individual items aren't somehow irrelevant, but they derive their real 'meaning' entirely from their collective orchestration into an overall 'effect', not from their singular placement; and in doing so become items with a quite different significance than they might otherwise possess on their own. And when it comes to the art of authentic artists – as defined here – it is the overall orchestrated effect which you have to grasp if you are to grasp the meaning of the individual works; you cannot properly understand individual artworks the other way around.

> **Illustration:** any example of distinctive, theme-based household décor, ie '1950s rock and roll jukebox-style interior design' : it is the overall effect which counts, not the individual items

In authentic art, as opposed to merely decorative, aesthetic craft, artists are using their artworks to represent a certain very distinctive and unusual 'take' on life. And it is this 'take' which is the art, not the individual artworks. And if you get the 'take' – if you are able to intuit it, or grasp it from the various individual artworks – then you understand the art, and any confusion as to the meaning and purpose and significance of individual pieces resolves itself. 'Art' then no longer appears to be the mysterious insertion of apparently non-traditional objects into a fine art context, it becomes a representation of a specific outlook, a specific 'cast of mind'; and the 'art' then reveals itself to be an intriguing glimpse into life and culture and experience through someone else's eyes.

'Art' has first to be 'curated' in order to become 'art'

So far we have been discussing, in a very general way, the key differences between 'art' and 'craft', emphasising that 'craft' is all about aesthetics, whereas 'art' is all about narrative, and mental perspective. In both cases, we are talking about presentational media; that is to say, media through which objects of various kinds, from the grossly physical to the wholly conceptual, are presented to an audience for appreciation. The presentational media are what are known as 'artforms', and these artforms are loose types of categorisation which help to give the audience a general idea of the type of material they might expect to be presented with.

And the concept of presentation is itself predicated on what can be described as the 'theatrical contract' or the 'theatrical pretence', meaning an implicit understanding between audience and agent that something is being presented for appreciation; and that this agreement or arrangement is essentially recreational rather than functional or utilitarian. We are all very familiar with the theatrical contract or pretence in everyday life, so much so that we are hardly aware of it, as it stretches from those moments when someone performs - knowingly to an audience - a simple act of skill in the kitchen or in the garden or in the street; to those more formal occasions when one settles into a chair to watch a television programme. These are situations in which we switch, in our perceptions, from one basic modality to quite another; that is to say, from an active engagement in life – working at something, thinking purposively about something – to a condition in which we 'sit back', relax, and merely observe.

The theatrical contract is well understood when we attend a specific event at a specific venue at a specific time, be it a concert, or a ballet, or a film. But this contract is hardly consciously acknowledged at all when we attend a gallery, or museum, even though it is as much in force as it would be in a concert hall. Implicit in a gallery presentation is the understanding that, everyone entering the gallery space is expected to switch from functional perceptions to appreciative ones, as the works are, in a very real sense, 'performing', though silently and without moving. The 'performance' can be largely decorative and aesthetic, or it can be narrative, inviting you into realms of immersive and imaginative thought; this is the essential presentational difference between objects merely crafted, and 'art proper'.

'Curation' as the moment something becomes 'art'

But before 'art' can be understood and appreciated as 'art', someone has to present it in a context where it will be understood as 'art', and not understood as fulfilling some other function. In other words, for 'art' to be 'art' in the very first instance, it has to be 'curated' as such; that is, deliberately and overtly situated by someone (the curator) in a context where the desired audience will knowingly understand that whatever is on display is presentational material, and not material of another kind. This may seem absurdly self-evident, but there are endless jokes about the possible confusion between artworks and things which are not artworks, stretching back to Duchamp's urinal 'Fountain' (1917)[21]; and today these confusions are simply the result of poor curating; that is to say, simply not making it apparent to all

---

[21] Duchamp's readymade is discussed at length later on in this book.

and sundry exactly where the art begins and ends.

> **Illustration: Duchamp's 'Fountain' (1917); not the first ever readymade, or the first example of re-contextualising an object into art, but a particularly famous one.**

Now it may appear at this stage that the idea of the curating of art – deliberately labelling something as art, and in so doing 'making' it art – is fraught with conceptual problems, not the least of which is an apparently uninformative circularity. Does curating mean that whatever is curated as art, becomes art ? Unfortunately not, because authentic 'art' possesses its own distinctive and substantial character, wholly different from other types of crafted material; and this means that art cannot be created or endowed with artistic qualities by mere decree: it has to possess certain meaningful characteristics to begin with. For something to be validly curated as 'art', it has to be more than just any old presentational material; it has to have a distinctive and substantial character of its own, so as to make it the meaningful subject of any audience appreciation. A mutually agreeable, evenly balanced relationship between curated artworks and their audience is essential if art is not to become a kind of dictatorship, imposed without justification on a bemused and sceptical public.

'Evenly-balanced' is the key factor in this relationship, but of course balance is not something that can be legislated for, or turned into some kind of dependable formula. Artists and curators have to be free to explore new possibilities, and to present as art materials and events which might not usually be considered art, but sooner or later there has to be some measure of 'vindication', whereby the art begins to justify itself as art. Currently this is not the case, and there is a widespread feeling in the general public – at least as reflected in online forums[22] – that much of what is being presented as art is not art at all, but shoddy workmanship dressed up as art. The public feels it is being made a fool of, and the professional interpreters of art – namely the critics – are not able to convince them otherwise, as they themselves are not a

---

[22] There are endless videos on YouTube in which 'modern art' is disparaged. Search, for example, for 'modern art is trash'.

hundred percent clear as to what is going on either.

Who qualifies as a 'curator' of art ?

Normally we think of a curator as someone in charge of a gallery, who curates – that is, organises and supervises exhibitions of artworks – in a publicly acknowledged professional capacity. But this is not the kind of very simple, ordinary and everyday 'curating' of art in question here: we are talking about the ability of anyone and everyone to take a particular object, or event, and by deliberately re-contextualising it - and somehow putting it on display - turning it into a presentational item, whether of aesthetic or artistic interest. We do this by finding a way to take it out of its functional usefulness, and giving it a new meaning, such that anyone looking at it will understand that it should be appreciated for its aesthetic or artistic qualities, rather than for any utilitarian purpose it might have. Any object can be displayed in this way, and anyone can curate such a display.

Common examples would be any items found in a household display cabinet. These items may be functioning tools and implements in another context – plates, glasses, guitars, clothing, and so on – and used as such, but as objects of display in a cabinet they are meant to be appreciated for their looks, and possibly for the imagery they invoke.

And when it comes to crafting specifically for display purposes, we take it as read that it is the craftsperson, or the artist, who decides on - or curates - the context within which their work is to be situated. By following certain rules, and by adhering to certain parameters, craftspeople can create works which conform to the requirements of their chosen artform, so they can then be readily appreciated as examples of that artform. Even in difficult cases, such as industrial noise being presented as music, we tend to go with the idea that it is the craftsperson's subjective 'intention' that is crucial to determining what they are trying to do, and how their work should be categorised, rather than a more objective criterion.

Most of the time, 'intention' – as an artist's 'self-categorising' and artistic validation of their own creations – can be accepted as a rule of thumb, at least in terms of a general direction of travel. If an artist declares, of a work, that it is 'meant to be art', we can, generally speaking, understand that it is meant to be something presentational, and not meant to be related to business, or sport, or religion, or some other possible categorisation. But as we have pointed out earlier, a declaration of intent alone cannot guarantee that a work is worthy of the label 'art', because art needs to possess certain specific characteristics, otherwise anything and everything could be art, and the label itself would have lost all currency. There have been those – including major artists - who have declared that 'everything is art' and 'everyone is an artist'[23], but this type of semi-mystical silliness may be fun to flirt with, but it doesn't advance any kind of meaningful understanding of art itself.

Any original creative intention can always be superseded by curation

A craftsperson may intend their created object to fulfil a certain purpose, but their conception of this purpose can always be overwritten by someone else who might want to claim it in the name of art. You can craft an object with the intention that it functions as a household implement, and someone else can come along and declare of that object that 'it's a work of art', re-contextualising it and giving it a new interpretation. The craftsperson might disagree and say 'No, it's not', but they can't prevent someone else from seeing it in that light. This particular line of argument may seem somewhat arcane right now, but as we shall see later, there are many cases – from Duchamp to anthropological art – where crafted material may initially have had a non-artistic purpose and function, yet later be legitimately 'curated' as art.

We continue to refer to 'art' in these discussions as if we have already clearly defined it - yet without having done so - and this makes much of what we have to say seem slightly suspect. But this is unavoidable in the sense that we are moving towards a definition both by peeling away the layers of mystical and magical thinking that currently go to make up the confused and confusing popular conception of art, and by listing those basic characteristics of art which cumulatively will move us in the right direction.

---

[23] Joseph Beuys, following Novalis, is one such; see for example Beuys's 1978 poster for the Free International University with the strapline 'Jeder Mensch Ein Künstler' (Tate Gallery, London).

Interim summary: aesthetic objects vs art objects

'Aesthetics' is all about the sensual – sensorial – pleasure to be derived from presentational crafted material. 'Presentational' objects are to be admired and appreciated for whatever qualities they possess, whether aesthetic or narrative, and are not objects of functional usefulness. Aesthetic objects strive to be beautiful, and sensorially attractive, whereas art objects present a type of narrative, and these narratives often have nothing to do with aesthetics, and don't have to be beautiful, attractive, or technically accomplished, to work their particular magic.

For art objects to take on their own distinctive presentational qualities, they have to be 'curated', that is to say, deliberately and meaningfully put into a context where they can be appreciated as 'presentational'. In other words, they have to be displayed as art objects, such that those viewing them understand them as 'art objects', and not objects of another kind.

But what are the 'distinctive presentational qualities' of an art object ? Given the wide range of material that artists and curators currently present as 'art' – especially as modern art – is it possible to tell the difference between art and not-art ?

We have reached the stage where the distinction between aesthetics and art has been clarified – up to a point – and it is now necessary to clarify the specific nature of art itself, such that anyone understanding it can easily tell the difference between art and everything else, as well being able to distinguish between good art and bad.

Understanding Modern Art

8

FOR ART TO BE DISTINCTIVELY ITSELF, IT HAS TO REVEAL "THE STRANGE AND THE DISTURBING"

What do we mean by 'art' as a form of narrative ? And what exactly is a 'narrative' in an artistic context ? An artistic narrative can be defined as the informational content contained in an artwork, above and beyond any aesthetic features present. If we disregard the sensorial beauty, attractiveness and accomplished technique manifest in a presentational object, what are we left with ? Most of the time, nothing in particular, which is why a lot of modern art is quite vacuous; but occasionally we stumble across a portal to another realm.

'Narrative' as regards art does not necessarily mean a sequential storyline, with a clear beginning, middle and end, involving characters engaged in realising a plot; though it does not preclude it. An artistic 'narrative' can mean joining – in a type of imaginative congruence – the mindset on display through a particular artwork, or collection of artworks by a particular artist; or it can mean inhabiting the imaginative landscape the artist is inviting you to enter through a symbolic work; or it can mean sharing in the 'take on life' the artist is revealing through their use of imagery. These are all variations on a basic idea, and that idea is that an authentic artwork is an entry point to a form of imaginative experience.

This might seem to be a very subtle angle on art, and perhaps counterintuitive, and calling for a kind of mental recalibration we are not familiar with, but this is far from the case: everyone is familiar with the narrative possibilities of everyday objects, from abstract symbolism – like a cross meaning religious suffering – to something more concrete – like a bunch of keys on the hall table meaning – let's say - the arrival of grandparents. In fact we probably spend infinitely more time with the narratives awakened in us by everyday objects than we do with the direct narratives of real people, and artistic narratives are really only an extension of this, though they present us, as we intend to argue, with information of a different order.

An artistic representation is not the same as reality itself: it is an abstraction away from reality

Everyday objects tell us everyday stories, stretching in a continuum from the delightful to the dreadful. Presentational objects, whether aesthetic or artistic, try to do more than show us what we already know, otherwise there would be little point in them. Aesthetic objects attempt to reveal to us aspects of beauty above and beyond that which we might encounter normally, and artistic objects attempt to engage us in narratives that would, as it were, take us on a journey to realms and perspectives we would not ordinarily come across. These realms and perspectives might have counterparts in the real world, but the point about 'art' is that it is presentational – that is, 're-presentational' – meaning that it is presented to you as a form of vicarious entertainment, or vicarious recreation. This is not to reduce art to the level of trivial diversion, or a relaxing distraction, merely giving us a rest from the serious business of succeeding in life: good art can be as profound and substantial as anything else we might experience, but we have to understand that presentational material is not of the same experiential order as everyday immersive experience, because art is essentially representational and therefore one step removed from reality, whereas ordinary life is direct and consequential in a way art can never be.

For example, the artistic representation of a crime is not the same thing as a real crime, and we as the art audience know instinctively where the dividing line is, even if the artistic representation is more compelling and enthralling than the real thing could ever be. This can seem surprising, but all it says is that certain types of imaginative experiences can capture the attention and unleash all kinds of emotions which real events fail to, though under normal circumstances we know that imaginative experiences of an artistic origin are not the same as real experiences, and that they can never be existentially superior to reality. Even when the death of a fictional character moves us more than the death of a member of our own family, we know within ourselves that this is simply a type of embarrassing anomaly, and that reality ought always to trump the imagination.

Ordinary narratives vs artistic narratives

There is a further important distinction which leads us, at last, directly to that which is distinctively 'art'. Conventional narratives, such as we might encounter in fairy tales, detective stories, romances, adventure stories, and so on, are always located within the wide boundaries of normal experience, stretching from the utterly commonplace to the unusual and the extraordinary. Conventional narratives are reassuring and heartening, even when they deal with extremes of behaviour and circumstance; they start with life as we know it, and in the end, whatever the twists and turns, return us to life as we know it.

Artistic narratives on the other hand, go beyond ordinary life as we know it, and reveal to us imaginative realms which we can somewhat loosely describe as the 'strange and disturbing'. This is their defining character, and the unique quality they bring to crafted presentational material, clearly distinguishing it from the ordinary, or the aesthetic. 'Art' proper is always characteristically strange and disturbing, and it can reveal this unfamiliar realm to us in a surprising number of ways.

'The strange and the disturbing'

Understanding 'art' depends on our ability to distinguish between the merely aesthetic – that is, the sensually beautiful – and the narratively artistic, which is about picking up on the perspectives and interior landscapes revealed to us through artworks, whether physical, or performative, or ideational. Artworks are therefore portals – entry points – to these 'narratives', or informational possibilities, or mental perspectives. Artworks are not necessarily linear narratives, like films or novels, but 'states of mind narratives', whereby the viewer, or the audience, picks up on the perspective or frame of mind on offer, and takes it on. That is the specific realm in which the art of any authentic artist is to be located; and it is never in the raw features of the artwork itself.

For example; you don't judge a film as a matter of the succession of images on the screen, or even on the narrative storyline; you judge it on its overall effect on you, that is to say, its overall impact on you as a 'totality', as a 'complete package'. And this somewhat mysterious imaginative totality is always 'located' at a level above and beyond the nuts and bolts of the film itself. And in exactly the same way, you don't judge a genuine artwork as if it were no more than the sum of its aesthetic features on display: genuine art only begins when you enter the realm the artist is inviting you into.

But the point about the artistic realm – as opposed to any other kind of presentational possibility – is that it has to be characteristically 'strange and disturbing' to qualify as authentically 'art'. What does this mean, exactly ? It means that 'art' is not just any kind of presentational material, and that the narrative contained within it can never be merely ordinary and familiar: art has to show you something you don't already know about, and with which you are not already familiar. And because the range of things we already 'know about' and are 'familiar with' stretches from reassuring domesticity to the horrors of war and crime, the distinctive capacity unique to art is that of revealing to us – presentationally and recreationally - the strange and the disturbing.

'Strange and disturbing' does not mean shocking and disgusting, or frightening and horrifying, or cruel and sadistic, or any of a range of negative and unpleasant emotions with which we are already well acquainted from everyday life. Strange and disturbing is a very particular type of revelation, and not necessarily always closely associated with the negative and the disagreeable; and its ability to disclose whole realms of imaginative possibilities is infinitely greater than those crafted presentations – usually cinematic – which have 'fear' or 'horror' or 'torture' or 'sex' as their central theme. And even in those instances where the films have been crafted to the highest aesthetic and narrative, 'negativity' on its own – without the 'strange and disturbing' to underpin and deepen its fascination – may be momentarily entertaining but is never profound or thought-provoking.

What do we mean by the 'strange and disturbing' ? We mean presentational material which seems to be mysteriously detached from the wide range of reassuring features we normally associate with everyday experience, and material which has found a way to undermine and unsettle them in some fascinating way, startling us into the sense that we have entered something equivalent to a parallel universe in which the familiar has been replaced by the uncanny. This doesn't have to involve a punch in the face; art can be subtle, and stealthy, and even, as we shall see in the case of Andy Warhol, paradoxical, and which in effect manages to 'celebrate the superficial in a profound way'!

Crafted presentational material that is merely beautifully and skilfully realised, even to the highest standards, can, when encountered in quantity, appear somewhat monotonous. This is because we can only take so much 'beauty' before it starts to lose its impact, and begins to appear to repeat itself; the reason being that the experience of sensorial beauty is almost entirely limited to its directness and immediacy, and it often fails to activate the imagination. It's not that beauty is skin deep – it's that aesthetic beauty is always contained – and limited – to a direct sensorial encounter with it.

Artistic material, on the other hand, while it may employ sensorial directness and immediacy as part of its overall orchestration of presentational options, only does so in the service of a much broader and more engaging mission, namely in presenting the viewer with an entry point to a realm of narrative experiences. Andy Warhol, for example, was wholly obsessed with the mechanics of a kind of sensational glitz and glamour, superficial and vacuous in the extreme, and his artworks might appear to respect the aspirations of aesthetics, but it would be quite mistaken to see his art as a feeble contemporary attempt at classicism: Warhol managed to create an entire universe of camp enchantment, a bizarre world of drug-addled nihilism, every bit as imaginatively immersive and extensive as that occupied by the cultural establishment.

Interim summary:
the conceptual trail from 'the beautiful', to 'the strange and the disturbing'

Crafted presentational material is anything which is intended to be admired and appreciated for its qualities, whether aesthetic and sensorial, or artistic and narrative. Presentational material is not intended to be functional or utilitarian, like tools and implements; rather it is intended to be 'on show' in a theatrical sense: you sit back and enjoy it.

Presentational material always has to be 'curated', meaning 'knowingly situated' in a context whereby everyone understands that it is 'presentational' as opposed to 'functional'.

Aesthetic presentational material aspires to be beautiful; artistic material aspires to engage with the imagination by means of subtle narratives. And in order for these subtle narratives to be distinctively artistic, as opposed to merely ordinary and everyday, they have to reveal something of 'the strange and the disturbing'.

9

WHAT DO WE WANT CRAFTED OBJECTS TO DO FOR US? AND WHAT DO WE WANT ART TO DO?

The conceptual trail we have followed so far begins with 'presentational material' – stuff we craft to look at and enjoy, and think about; that is, stuff which is non-utilitarian – and presentational material can then be subdivided into 'beautiful stuff' and 'narrative stuff'. Beautiful stuff is decorative and aesthetic; narrative stuff is about showing us unusual realms of our imaginative capacities. Narrative stuff can be ordinary and familiar; but it can also be artistic, that is to say, strange and disturbing.

The point about this particular conceptual trail is that it has a certain sequential logicality to it, in that it moves step by step from the primitive crafting of tools and implements for survival and for the needs of everyday life, to the more recreational and theatrical possibilities when we stand back – or more likely, sit back – and 'think about things' in the more philosophical and reflective terms of 'life and existence and human destiny'. This particular sequence is underpinned by the idea of a 'hierarchy of needs' of the kind outlined by Maslow, and there is a certain self-evidence to the whole progression from basic physical needs to more cerebral, contemplative ones.

And for the sake of conceptual contrast, with the aim of trying to expose weaknesses in this line of thinking, we can try another angle on the whole question of 'art', and frame it in terms of what it is, exactly, we want these various non-utilitarian crafted objects to do for us; or put slightly differently, what purpose are they meant to fulfil ? For this line of questioning to work – meaning to have it usefully clarify the whole idea of 'art' – we would have to assume that the public at large already have a clear idea what art is, so they are able to approach it – in its various manifestations – armed with meaningful expectations. Otherwise we end up in the peculiar situation where people engage with art, and are prepared to spend time and money on it, without really knowing what it is they are up to, except in a very obvious and uninformative sense.

And if we try to make sense of 'art' by looking at what people think they are getting out of it, we run the very real risk of being forced to derive the principles of art and craft from ideas which are themselves confused, and mistaken, and perhaps even plain wrong. 'Thinking about art' is always in danger of descending into 'art mysticism', where people enter a frame of mind in which thoughts and feelings they have decided are what art is all about, become the basis for their opinions and whole way of approaching the subject.

But if we stick with this approach for now, and embrace the realms of 'art mysticism' for what it can tell us about what people want out of art, we can still usefully sort various approaches to art into clear and distinct categories. And we can see that, in many ways, many people treat art quasi-religiously, as if it were a personal source of meaning to them, a 'state of mind' which they can dip into whenever they want, and which hopefully affords them a fulfilling sense of meaning and purpose – at least momentarily.

Art as social and political activism

This is where presentational crafting is employed in the service of social and political agendas, ranging from non-commercial advertising, to satirical cartooning. Propaganda posters are well-known features of totalitarian regimes, whether Marxist or fascist, and the chosen imagery is designed to drive home a message of one sort or another, usually of an inspirational, motivational character. Crude caricature – of the kind that would supposedly break the spirit of the enemy – is the weapon of choice of the insurgent activist in modern society, though in all cases the crafting itself is only ever a means to a non-aesthetic end; meaning, presumably, that if there were a more effective way of getting the message across, posters and political 'art' would be abandoned in favour of some other form of activism.

For our purposes, the point about being an artist activist is that it allows one's crafting to take on a mystical meaning – such as working towards a greater good, or working towards the betterment of the society in general – which the self-image of being a 'mere craftsperson' does not really permit. Visualising oneself as a political artist, and taking on the establishment for the best of reasons, in turn can sustain an ongoing inner sense of relevance and excitement, and these beliefs go some way to answering deep seated existential needs for meaning and purpose.

The key occupational hazard of the politically-committed craftsperson is that of the unfortunately close relationship between the impact of one's imagery, and their ephemerality. In other words, the greater the impact of an image on its target audience – as a function of the image's absolute appropriateness at that moment in time – the greater the chance that, once the moment has passed, the imagery will lose almost all of its meaning, and become an empty shell.

Art as a 'spiritual calling'

Some artists like to think that the feelings and sensations aroused by their contact with presentational material are essentially refined, and elevated, and therefore 'spiritual'. This is of a piece with the orchestration of sensations in religious art – such as standing in speechless awe before a classical oil painting of a bible scene, or responding to the massive and imposing architectural presence of a religious building – and the idea that specific forms of 'art' can connect one with refined and elevated states of mind has widespread acceptance across many cultures. But as in the much more secular and seemingly trivial political art, the presentational crafting itself is only ever a means to an end – namely spiritual experience – and presumably if there were a more effective way to achieve the same thing, then we could jettison the art.

Art as 'unknown and unknowable'

Insofar as 'art' remains undefined and indistinct, and a source of vague feelings of connectedness with refined states of mind, and elevated perceptions, 'art' will continue to be cherished as the realm where finer feelings are validated – at least for a time – in a mystical though not necessarily religious way. In other words, 'art' is a realm where I can think all sorts of thoughts, and have all kinds of feelings, and no one can, or will, contradict me. Art can be a private refuge, where I am free to let myself go, imaginatively speaking; though, as is the case with most instances of solipsism, we do want to share our impressions with others, and have them validated socially.

But as things stand, with the persisting confusion as to what 'art' might be in itself - if anything at all - there are many good reasons why people would actively *want* to keep 'art' in a realm of the unknown, and unknowable. We don't want to discover that our finer feelings are not particularly spiritual or significant, and that our perceptual acuity is not all that acute, and that our taste in matters of taste is just plain tasteless. So we feel oddly reassured when a professorial talking head declares that 'no one really knows what art is'.

Where does this leave us ? It leaves us back where we started, with the obstinate phenomenon of 'art mysticism', wherein presentational crafting becomes an option people like to embrace for sources of meaning, and purpose, and a sense of refined wellbeing. 'Art' is by no means the only realm within which people can validate themselves in this way – there is also religion, and politics, and social and environmental activism – but 'art' appeals to those who are perceptually sensitive and responsive. And in a world in which leisure time becomes more available, art is likely to become ever more important as a source of recreational engagement.

But what exactly is it that we want presentational material – aesthetic and artistic – to do for us ? We want it to achieve for us, in its own unique way, an aesthetically pleasurable lived environment – architecturally and decoratively – and beyond that, opportunities for recreational enjoyment and entertainment – concerts, ballets, performances, exhibitions, films. Sensual, aesthetic pleasure is one thing, but it can only go so far, because we also want to be stimulated imaginatively, and this is where narrative presentations come into their own. Everyday narratives, whether conversational or presentational, reveal to us aspects of the world with which we are already familiar; artistic narratives show us aspects of the strange and disturbing, and take us to places we might not otherwise be able to reach. Art, of course, is also radically different from ordinary life in that it is essentially vicarious, and at least one step removed from reality through a process of artistic abstraction.

More importantly, 'art', as our vicarious access to strange and disturbing narratives, is our only means to these realms, short of our having to encounter strange and disturbing events in real life. Art allows us to contemplate and consider – in a paradoxically pleasurable and fulfilling way – dreadful and uncanny possibilities which might be too much for us in the flesh. Yes there are those artists who, in immersive performances, try to blur the distinction between the vicarious and the real, but when you think about it you can see that this is just another orchestrated artifice, and really no more than a technical, if alarming, gimmick: no immersive performance has ever intentionally injured a member of the audience, even if, in the case of extreme performers like Marina Abramović and Chris Burden, they deliberately injure themselves.

Now there are those who, for whatever reason, simply don't accept an account of 'art' which reaches beyond the aesthetic and into the narrative. And while they might accept that some artforms employ narratives as their essential medium, the idea that 'art' itself exists in a realm above and beyond the manifest aesthetic features and possibilities commonly associated with a particular form seems unreasonable and counterintuitive. Paintings are paintings, and music is music - so the argument goes - and what you encounter is what you get; to look elsewhere for meaning or significance is to intellectualise a situation which doesn't call for it. Art is supposedly about the feelings and sensations generated by a direct contact with works of art.

But this doctrine of sensorial aestheticism - when compared to the idea of art as a narrative realm - is surprisingly shallow and restricted. It reduces all encounters with every type of art in every type of artform to instances of 'the beautiful', and while there are infinite varieties of 'the beautiful', and infinite occasions in which it can manifest itself, it is far from the only experiential possibility open to the onlooker. There is, for a blindingly obvious start, everything which is 'not beautiful' and 'not attractive' and 'not classically museum-worthy'; and the idea that these artistic possibilities have 'nothing to say' and 'nothing to tell us' shows how blinkered and vacuous the aesthetics of beauty can be. There are of course those critics and commentators who describe even deeply repellent works of art as 'beautiful' – and in so doing incorporate them into the monotonous categories of orthodox aesthetics – but this should be seen for the intellectual disability that it is. If everything in art is only about 'the beautiful', then what does that say for us as experiencing beings with minds capable of a vast range of responses ?

Art must surely reveal to us vicarious realms beyond the merely 'aesthetically beautiful'. It can only do this if the experiential categories are expanded to include possibilities other than the merely attractive, and without simply substituting another form of aesthetic restriction for the one we already have in place. We have to concede that as human beings we are essentially predisposed to the positive, and to the optimistic, and to the happy ending, and that we would recoil from a sensorial aesthetics focussed on the unpleasant and dreadful, yet these are realms we can enjoyably tackle 'narratively', through the kind of open-ended theatrical experiences some artists are able to present us with. Think of the many enjoyably horrific films and novels, for a start.

Interim summary:
art can do more than confine us to 'the beautiful'

What do we want presentational material to do for us ? For most people, including art professionals, art is about the decorative and the aesthetically beautiful. Some modern artists like to describe art as being about 'interesting ideas', as if art were popular conversational philosophy by different means, but very often even these people find themselves unable to reach beyond an aesthetics of 'the beautiful'. But art can be shown to have narrative possibilities which are far more engaging and interesting than the merely 'beautiful', and which open up to the viewer entirely different realms of imaginative and experiential opportunities.

The essence of art: presentational material which discloses and reveals

In its essence, what art does is reveal – or disclose – to us realms of vicarious imaginative experience we could not reach any other way. Showing us realms of experience with which we are already familiar does not disclose anything; at best it reassures us, or confirms in us things we already know, so for art to do something which is distinctively artistic, it will have to disclose to us the strange and the disturbing and the uncannily unusual. We can, in a way, arrive at this conclusion by a process of elimination: what would be the point of art if not to reveal to us – recreationally – those things with which we are unfamiliar and of which we are unaware ?

Understanding Modern Art

10

PROBLEMS WITH THIS DEFINITION- PARADOXES AND OBJECTIONS

What we have tried to argue thus far is that 'art', as a distinctive presentational quality quite separate from aesthetics, is basically a form of narrative theatre, using the features and opportunities provided by any artform to reveal an unusual type of 'story', although not necessarily of a sequential, plot-driven sort. By 'narrative' we mean that the artist is presenting a perspective, or inner landscape, or experiential 'world', and inviting the viewer, or listener, to join them in an immersive, vicarious experience. The whole point of authentic art is that it offers a form of open-ended recreational theatre, allowing the viewer to explore the strange and disturbing aspects of life in a controlled environment. Art is about picking up on the 'artistic narrative' that is being offered to you – by an artwork, or collection of them – and then grasping it.

Now the most obvious objection to our definition is that all we have done is take an ambiguous word – 'art' – and given it a meaning according to our wishes, and against the prevailing usage, namely that of 'art' meaning 'beautifully crafted objects according to classical standards'. 'Art', according to popular usage – and this includes art professionals – doesn't really have a fixed meaning, and can more or less mean anything you want it to mean. So 'art' is what you make it; it's a matter of taste, and subjective judgement, and if it had a distinctive core to it, someone would have discovered that essence a long time ago, and the endless questions as to 'what is art ?' and 'is this art ?' would have been settled by now.

But this assumes – on a dogmatic conservatism – that there is nothing to be gained from clarifying the concept of art, and that there is nothing wrong with the superficial reduction of art to a matter of taste and subjectivity, underpinned by an aesthetic of beauty. It is obvious to anyone who visits galleries regularly, or who takes an interest in modern art, that classical aesthetic theory centred on ideas of 'the beautiful' cannot make the least sense of modern artworks, and is constantly reduced to trying to find something 'beautiful' or 'intellectually interesting' about them. In classical terms, modern art is simply a form of insurgent silliness and student japery, coupled with a total absence of technical skill.

The problem is that classical aesthetics – insofar as it translates into the direct experience of artworks - is always heading toward something like a high camp sensuality – a fey 'attempted ecstasy' – in that it has nowhere else to go. Once you've concluded that a Caravaggio is 'magnificent' and 'sublime', and 'gorgeous', and once you've acknowledged the undoubted technical mastery on display, what else is there to do but attempt a kind of mystical swooning, giving yourself over to waves of subtle aesthetic pleasure ? This kind of refined sensoriality invites direct comparison with the noises of the gourmet tucking into a dish of subtle flavours, and the only thing that can rescue these events from seeming more than a little indecent is to attempt to sublimate them in a civilising gloss. This doesn't mean that sensual pleasure is forbidden, or that disgusting indecency can't be delightful; it's simply to recognise it for what it is – a limited and limiting sensoriality, and neither profound nor spiritual nor elevated – and then to recognise that the imaginative possibilities afforded by narrative art go way beyond swooning at a Masaccio or grunting on a truffle.

Put differently, the whole point about spending some time clarifying the nature of art is that, in terms of the definition being put forward here, it greatly enhances the encounter with art itself by revealing an entire 'realm' of narrative, imaginative possibilities, rather than restricting the experience of art to aesthetic sensoriality. Experiencing different ways of thinking, and inhabiting different perspectives and different interior landscapes is a far more interesting undertaking than refining one's sense of 'beauty'; and the only way we can experience these different worlds – vicariously, recreationally, and in a context which encourages reflection and contemplation – is through art.

This is not a definition 'by decree'

It is important to emphasise that our definition of 'art' as 'presentational crafting which characteristically reveals the strange and disturbing' is not a definition by decree: we are not laying down the law, or imposing a definition from above, and refusing to acknowledge other possibilities. Nor is this a matter of what we *want* 'art' to be, and so twisting the facts in our favour. Our definition is predicated on the idea that, when all else has been given a fair voice, this is what art actually *is in itself* - as something quite particular to itself - and something quite other than aesthetics and the quest for beauty.

We arrived at this definition by trying to find a rationale for the extraordinary goings-on in modern art, such that the account would be both respectful – meaning treating modern art as a valid and substantial pursuit on its own terms, and not merely as a student jape – and, infinitely more importantly, *explanatory* – meaning that it would explain, in a convincing and objective way, what modern art was really trying to do, when given the opportunity to realise itself. A consequence of this would necessarily be that if modern art possessed objective characteristics, which could be identified by any interested party, then it follows that it ought to be possible to judge the good from the bad, even in those cases when such a judgement conflicted directly with one's own likes and dislikes. In other words, it ought to be possible to acknowledge good art – art which is good at what it does, namely insofar as it presents a portal to a strange and disturbing world – even if you don't like what you are being presented with. It goes without saying that this type of thinking is a world away from the subjective, whimsical, prejudicial and high camp domain of aesthetics.

How then to explain modern art ? It clearly can't be done by reference to theories of aesthetic beauty which, after all, have their own parameters and refinements and are determined by sensory predilections; and this means that 'art', if it is to mean anything at all, will have to be located in a realm other than that of 'the logic of the beautiful'. One idea which has fairly widespread acceptance – though it has never quite replaced the aesthetics of beauty as the ultimate arbiter of art – is the idea that art – especially modern art - is all about 'interesting ideas', or 'making you think', or 'showing you things differently'; this appears to turn art into an educative device of the sort you might encounter at a progressive primary school, where the teacher holds up an unusual object for the class to brainstorm.

'Art' as 'brainteasing' is somewhat more relevant to explaining modern art than 'art as beauty', but the implication here is that, ultimately, modern artists are just people who craft their brainteasers into artworks rather than writing them down or turning them into crosswords and magazine puzzles. Appreciating art is then a matter of decoding the puzzle, and art ends with the 'aha !' moment, beyond which there is not much else to say or think about, and although this is a popular method of explaining the supposed 'meaning' of an artwork – just listen to the docents at a nearby gallery - it makes art itself seem a very trivial undertaking, and hardly worth the effort. Why bother with art when you can do real puzzles instead ?

The theory that the idea of 'art' is part of a 'language game', and therefore has no fixed meaning

The 'language game' theory, formulated by Ludwig Wittgenstein[24], proposes that certain words derive their meaning entirely from their use in a specific context, and as the context changes, so the meaning of the word changes. Wittgenstein illustrated his theory with the idea of the 'family resemblance', where many very different people, all genetically members of the same family, and all manifesting certain family features, can also manifest differences as well. No single physical characteristic is shared by all, yet everyone shows one or other family trait.

Wittgenstein employed the word 'game' to illustrate the idea of 'family resemblance' at work in our use of language: all sorts of very different activities are called 'games', from tiddlywinks to rugby, and from family squabbles to the living of life itself; the only way we can know what the word 'game' means

---

[24] Especially in the 'Philosophical Investigations' (2001).

in any utterance is to know it's meaning specific to that utterance.

The 'language game' theory is very popular with professional philosophers, and with many others, including philosophers of art, because it's one of those theories like 'life is what you make it' or 'God helps those who help themselves' which give you licence to do whatever it is you want without having to think too deeply about it. It puts the matter of defining 'art' with any clarity and specificity to bed, and is therefore done with it, in perpetuity. But it doesn't dispense with theorising as such, and so theoreticians to come up with any theory they like: after all, who's to say that my flatulent speculations don't have a 'family resemblance' to some kind of truth ?

But if we have genuine suspicion that, for all its silliness, modern art might actually be a distinct activity in its own right, and not just be a laughable attempt at classicism, then the hunt is on. What are these people – the modern artists – up to ? If we could identify something distinctive that only they were doing, which in turn would explain, lucidly, how to understand what they were doing, what might we find ? This is the logic we have pursued here.

The problem with popular usage

Perhaps the most difficult aspect of the definition of 'art' we are proposing is that it runs counter to the way people want to use the word 'art' in ordinary speech, which means that even if the definition were to be accepted, it would be almost impossible to get people to replace the word 'art' with the words 'skilfully crafted', or 'aesthetically crafted', or words to that effect. People like to use the word 'art' to describe anything crafted that has a special quality to it, and which somehow elevates it above mere workmanship. 'Art' seems to be a more creative, resonant, and evocative label than 'craft', and this is why people like to refer to 'his art' or 'her art' to describe work – even non-presentational crafting – which seems to have a certain extra zing to it.

'Art' as 'creatively and imaginatively crafted' therefore pulls the meaning away from 'narratively strange and disturbing' and perpetuates the confusion between aesthetics and art proper. It also reflects the possibility – which will be explored in detail later – that, insofar as people are happy enough with art as the specialised activity which results in a decorated, ornamented and attractive environment, they are not much interested in delving into the realms of altered perspectives and unfamiliar interior landscapes. In other words, art is, for many people, only about 'advertising' and 'interesting architecture' and not much else; and if you want more than that you can go to museums, and if you want even more than that you can visit modern art galleries, but what goes on in such places is so remote from the everyday 'concerns of the street' as to be not worth considering.

So, then, how come this conception of art isn't more widely known and understood ?

Another kind of objection to our definition of art can be framed in terms of popularly-held ideas of 'likelihood' and 'probability'. If our idea is as cogent as we claim it is, why hasn't anyone else come up with it ? Why does it seem vaguely counterintuitive, going against popularly-held beliefs ?

The reasons for this are complex, and fall into two important categories. Firstly, as has been said before, conceptual clarity is not considered important in the experience of art – art is something you first engage with directly, and think about later; and the consensus is that it doesn't much matter what you think about art, no one is going to contradict you. People may not share your subjective opinions about particular artists or particular genres, but when it comes to art in general, it's very much a free-for-all as regards definitions and clarifications. Even in scholarly and academic circles, there is no agreed definition of art, and there is certainly no concerted effort to arrive at one.

Secondly –and perhaps more judgementally – none of the big names in art criticism, and those who could make a difference in making art more objective and less opinionated, seem able to make the necessary shift from an explanation of the aesthetics of art objects, to a more encompassing view of the 'art of an artist' which grasps the perspectival underpinning of that art. And it's not as if these concepts are unfamiliar and unavailable to them, but they don't seem to want to acknowledge and appreciate them, and in doing so come to a more interesting and disclosing view of art than one which subliminally always disparages those who display less than sumptuous classical aesthetic technique. There are plenty of studies which are titled 'The Art of ...', or 'The World of...' which appear to acknowledge the importance of an underlying perspective uniting an entire oeuvre, yet these apparently encompassing views tend always to be betrayed in the detail, in that the critic is unable to articulate, with any confidence, this 'broader underlying perspective', and so is forced to return to the aesthetics of individual artworks.

In other words, art critics are either unwilling or unable to 'understand' art as that which underpins and illumines an entire approach, rather than that which manifests in the features of single objects. 'The art of Andy Warhol' is Warhol's specific and distinctive artistic take on life, not simply the characteristic features of his individual artworks. If you want to understand Warhol, you have to be able to join him – vicariously – in his take on life and art, rather than start trying to explain the relationship between his minimalist and shoddy aesthetics and say, classical oil paintings. Art critics don't seem to want to do this, and art criticism is all the poorer for it. We will discuss this in greater detail in a later chapter, with specific examples of underpowered art criticism.

Understanding Modern Art

PRACTICE

Understanding Modern Art

11

HOW DOES OUR NEW CONCEPTION OF ART IMPROVE ON THE OLD?

The popular conception of 'art' as a vague, largely irreconcilable mishmash of ideas about 'beauty' and 'new ways of seeing things' always leaves the viewer – professional or amateur – wondering how to interpret anything modern and unfamiliar. The default position is, of course, always to look for a quality which could be described, in the loosest possible sense, as 'beautiful'; and if not beautiful then, in a casual and conversational sense, as 'interesting'. And if these elements, or something which could approximate to them, can be found, then the viewer most likely feels emboldened to 'go with their feelings' and judge the modern artwork as a combination of mystical predilections – that is to say, intimately held intuitions regarding crafted things – and whatever resonances their memories throw up.

As has been said before, no one seems to be particularly worried by this state of affairs. Painters go on painting; sculptures go on sculpting; performers go on performing; critics go on criticising; and the art market continues to generate hundreds of millions of dollars for people in the right places. And more to the point, thousands happily wander around art galleries when they have an afternoon off, as well as occasionally watching programmes about art if one catches their notice.

What we have been trying to do is cut through all this casual, care-for-nothing muck and try to get to the point of art, especially of modern art, which, as anyone with the least interest in the subject can confirm, is deeply perplexing. If modern art is not to remain a feeble, semi-mystical bit of fluff, then it has to be clarified such that we know what artists are trying to do – even if they don't consciously know themselves – so we can separate success and failure, and the good from the bad. We need to be able to rely on objective principles, not on subjective whims. Anything less is a conceptual and intellectual failure.

The conceptual trail we have followed began with a separation of human crafting into the simplest of elemental categories, showing how all forms of crafting always represent responses to specific human needs, from the basics of food and safely, all the way up to the recreational and the spiritual. When we reach the recreational state of crafting – above and beyond sports and games – we are no longer talking about making and using functional tools and implements; instead we are talking about 'presentational' material, which people are expected to respond to contemplatively, and reflectively. And in this realm, aesthetic needs are met by finding ways to actualise beauty, whether in decorating the environment, or in crafting works which manifest attractiveness and sensorial appeal. Beyond aesthetics we have the desire for recreational narratives, and these fall into two essential though not exclusive categories – the 'merely diverting' on the one hand, and the artistic on the other. Ordinary narratives are merely amusing and entertaining; artistic narratives, although also vicariously entertaining in their own special way, explore the strange and disturbing.

Now if we accept that these very simple and elemental categories are accurate, then we are in a strong position to separate that which is 'authentically art' from that which is merely 'attempted art', or, more charitably, merely 'creative crafting'. If we investigate and explore what the artworks are telling us, then it is relatively easy to see whether or not they possess an artistic message – a message which takes us to unusual and odd realms of experience – or merely a creatively crafted message, diverting and entertaining perhaps, but nothing narratively unusual or strange. Joseph Beuys takes us well into the strange, and is therefore an authentic artist; Tracey Emin - insofar as she is just presenting us with endless aspects of her chaotic life, and although a very successful self-publicising craftswoman (a 'show-woman', if you like) - is decidedly not; Jeff Koons is managing to be both disturbingly banal as well as relentlessly so, and this certainly qualifies him as an artist; Ai Weiwei makes spectacular and interesting displays, wholly based in aesthetics, and they don't reveal anything we didn't already know. Steven Spielberg is a master filmmaker, and undoubtedly a superb craftsman, but his films – except for moments in Duel (1971) – are never more than diverting entertainment; David Lynch, on the other hand, is clearly an artist.

Abstract vs narrative art

Now we can see at a stroke from this that abstract art is not really art at all, but creative crafting, based almost wholly in aesthetics. 'Almost', because it is possible to use abstract imagery in the service of narratives, but the narrative would already have to be in place for the abstract image to have any narrative meaning, so we can conclude from this that the more detached from narrative an image is in itself, the less it has to do with art, and the more it is really no more than an instance of decorative craft.

This of course runs directly counter to the idea of according 'deep meaning' and 'conceptual significance' to abstract painting, when in fact the canvases are clearly no more than colours and shapes. It is possible to discuss the aesthetics of abstraction, and trace different styles and methods, but this is aesthetics at its most flimsy and rarefied[25], and outside the realm of environmental decorating would seem to be a waste of time: after all, the very concept of artistic abstraction is founded on the idea of breaking away from conventional parameters such as narrative and identifiable content, and if you dispense with them you are only left with bare compositional elements; and in the case of painting these can only ever be shape and colour.

Abstraction is the final phase of artistic distortion and distancing, in that everything becomes so remote from everyday objects as to be unrecognisable, and therefore ultimately without narrative possibility. Distortion is of course an essential capacity in any presentational crafting, but

---

[25] See for example the absurdist ramblings of Clement Greenberg (2006) on the supposedly profound ideas underpinning abstract art.

it has to be orchestrated in such a way that it does not cross over into unrecognizability, and thereby lose its potential narrative significance. Picasso showed what can be done with distortion in 'The Weeping Woman' (1937),

> **Illustration: Pablo Picasso's 'The Weeping Woman' (1937) in the Tate Modern, London**

but by the time we reach De Kooning's "Woman" (1949-1950) etc series, we are reaching the end of the narrative line, and collapsing into mere noise:

> **Illustration: Willem de Kooning 'Woman' series, c1950s; any examples**

   This kind of elimination of 'narrative' through abstraction is a particular problem in painting and sculpture, which some craftspeople have attempted to circumvent by giving their works narratively specific titles, for example Joan Mitchell in 'City Landscape' (1955):

> **Illustration: Joan Mitchell 'City Landscape' (1955)**

but this only demonstrates the limits of the medium itself.

   However, we need to make clear that it is not only the visual imagery of abstract expressionism which is artistically null and void, it is also the lack of 'art' underpinning it. Mitchell's works, like those of De Kooning and Pollock and Rothko and any number of other big names in abstract art, are not portals to strange realms of perspective or the imagination, they are simply dabblings in aesthetics, attempting to find new ways to express beauty and attractiveness by exploring the outer limits of shape and colour. They have their own significance in the history of aesthetics, and can be admired as examples of creative crafting, but they offer nothing beyond visual sensation.

   Why is this ? Because none of these painters found a way –

deliberately or inadvertently – to connect to narrative possibilities that went beyond aesthetics. As things stand, their work cannot be curated – that is, deliberately contextualised by someone – as 'art', because nothing in what they did or produced or said leads anywhere other than to colour and shapes on a canvas. If, for example, Joan Mitchell had said that her paintings – including their seemingly innocent titles – were attempts to ward off an unseen alien presence, and that she was following a visual language that came to her in fragments during episodes of interdimensional possession, we would suddenly be relocated in a fascinating and intriguing realm – a genuinely artistic landscape – but as it is, Joan Mitchell was just trying to be a good painter and paint aesthetically meaningful works.

Some of the extremes of modern art now make sense: Duchamp's 'Fountain' (1917), again

More than anything else, a theory of 'art' as a very particular type of strange and disclosing 'narrative realm' makes sense of some of the seemingly absurd examples of modern art in a way no other theory can convincingly do, as well as also offering a means to discriminate between good and bad art; in other words, between successful attempts at art, and those less so.

We can start with Duchamp's 'Fountain' (1917), and work outward from there. The story goes that Duchamp submitted a readymade urinal as an artwork – as something of a Dadaist joke – to an art exhibition in New York; and although the work was rejected, Duchamp and his circle were able, through writings and publicity, to turn the whole situation to their advantage, and make it something of an 'artistic statement', promoting ideas about breaching conservatism, artistic narrowness, and all the rest of it.

It's not clear from the historical facts either what actually happened – one account has it that the urinal wasn't Duchamp's idea[26] – or what Duchamp and others were actually trying to achieve with this 'action'. We also need to bear in mind that 'Fountain' wasn't the first readymade artwork by any

---

[26] It is worth pursuing the whole story in detail - through Wikipedia and articles elsewhere - just as an interesting example of how difficult it is to get at the facts of any particular piece of 'artistic history'.

means – Duchamp and the Dadaists had been producing them for years[27] – but it was certainly the one that captured people's attention, despite the fact that it wasn't exhibited at the exhibition it was intended for.

And we can't be sure what the original 'artistic intention' was; nor would our knowing that offer us an authoritative and definitive explanation as to the events themselves. But what we can say in hindsight is that someone – presumably Duchamp – decided to present (curate) the urinal as an object of presentational crafting, such that gallerygoers could 'encounter' it – that is, to engage with it – as they would any other presentational work. This is a technical way of saying that, at least as far as the logic of presentational crafting is concerned, Duchamp was going along with the whole system as it stood.

It's not difficult to see why Duchamp's urinal caused confusion, in that it toyed with basic notions of sculptural aesthetics, without wholly dismissing them. It was a sculpture of a sort, after all, even if not a typical art studio production. It had its own aesthetic qualities, though these related to the logic of utilitarian design rather than of sculptural beauty. There is also the obvious element of humour, undermining convention by lampooning it. But the most difficult idea for the traditionalist to come to terms with is that Duchamp didn't physically craft the piece in any orthodox way, but simply wandered into a shop and bought it 'readymade' off the shelf; although he did scrawl 'R. Mutt 1917' on its side as a way of personalising it as an object. And as a form of sculptural possibility, readymades threatened the very foundations of artistic originality and the nurturing of skilful craft.

But having confounded common expectations, what then ? Is simple aesthetic confusion the end of the Duchamp story ? The situation can be clarified by applying our basic set of interpretative principles: what happened was that, whatever the various intentions, and whatever the interpretative responses, and whatever the ultimate historical details, the Dadaist readymade introduced – or rather occasioned – a significant new avenue of narrative possibility into the visual arts, and in so doing radically altered the course of art itself. But is this what someone like Duchamp intended ? Probably not; it was likely just another Dadaist stunt – a conceptual joke – which over time would likely have been swept away by the forces of conservatism. But does it matter that he and his circle did not really know what they were doing ? Once again, no: they were playing games with the basic

---

[27] See books on the history of Dada, eg Dachy (2006) p.70.

principles of presentational material; and in toying with these conceptual parameters, something new emerged, perhaps by chance, or luck.

And what was the possibility that emerged ? Basically that objects of presentational crafting might be items in a theatrical landscape, rather than articles of strictly aesthetic interest. Artworks might be portals to imaginative worlds, rather than merely beautiful objects, to be admired solely for their sensorial qualities. But does Duchamp's urinal lead us into anything that could be called a 'theatrical landscape', and if so, of what sort ? 'Fountain', isolated on its own, is no more characteristically 'art' than any random object singled out for curation or presentation; but it becomes art when you look further into the kind of presentational world that Duchamp was populating with other artworks such as 'Bottle-Rack' (1914), 'Bicycle Wheel' (1963) and the snow shovel 'In Advance of the Broken Arm'(1915).

> **Illustration: examples of Duchamp's readymades: 'Bottle-Rack' (1914), 'Bicycle Wheel' (1963) and the snow shovel 'In Advance of the Broken Arm'(1915).**

We could try to argue here, as many have done, that Duchamp was a 'conceptual' artist, and therefore concerned with 'interesting ideas' and getting people to 'see things differently'. The Metropolitan Museum of Art in New York explains on their website:

> "By World War I, he had rejected the work of many of his fellow artists as "retinal" art, intended only to please the eye. Instead, Duchamp wanted, he said, "to put art back in the service of the mind."
>
> ...He wanted to distance himself from traditional modes of painting in an effort to emphasize the conceptual value of a work of art, seducing the viewer through irony and verbal witticisms rather than relying on technical or aesthetic appeal. The object became a work of art because the artist had decided it would be designated as such.
>
> ...By pushing and ultimately transgressing such boundaries within the art world, Duchamp's works reflected the artist's sensibility. His use of irony, puns,

alliteration, and paradox layered the works with humor while still enabling him to comment on the dominant political and economic systems of his time.

...A prolific artist, his greatest contribution to the history of art lies in his ability to question, admonish, critique, and playfully ridicule existing norms in order to transcend the status quo—he effectively sanctioned the role of the artist to do just that."[28]

But as we have argued earlier, treating art as 'amateur philosophy by visual means' is a deeply trivialising approach, and the idea of playful visual puns and wry humour as the endpoint of presentational crafting is dispiriting to say the least. There's nothing essentially wrong with intellectualising art and finding ways to employ cerebral concepts in the service of some greater narrative, and this may well have been what Duchamp thought he was doing. In later life he supposedly renounced art for chess – playing chess presumably being what he believed to be heavy cerebral activity – but when dealing with someone who has long inhabited the presentational world, and is very familiar with its duplicity, we can't be sure that literal meanings apply. Either way, Duchamp's statement about wanting to "to put art back in the service of the mind" is probably best understood as an art-mystical indulgence on his part, a method whereby he was organising and explaining his ideas as best he could.

Put plainly, Duchamp – in common with very many other artists – didn't really have a convincing explanation for what he was doing, or what his works meant – and he probably wasn't sure himself – but this doesn't mean that he wasn't able to produce convincing art. You don't have to have a clear conception of a skill to be an expert practitioner of it; nor do you need to be able to articulate your craft lucidly to be able to apply it – practice comes first, and understanding later.

So to find the sense and meaning underpinning Duchamp's art, we have to take a look at the Duchampian artistic landscape as a whole – Duchamp's exteriorisation of his inner perspective – and see if it reveals to us a convincing world of its own – a strange and unsettling take on life – which would thereby qualify it as 'art'. And one of the easiest ways to do this is simply to flip through a book on an artist's work and see if the combination of representative images alerts one to the presence of an unusual and uncanny vision; and this is certainly the case with Duchamp: he leads us straight into a

---

[28] Nan Rosenthal, on the Metropolitan Museum's Duchamp webpage.

peculiarly dehumanised realm populated by odd contraptions and things which look like they want to be machines of a sort; and Duchamp's paintings – those of the brownish hue – are advanced cubist sketches alluding perhaps to mechanical movement, or the abstract representations of entrapped and contained activity. There is also a hint of cruelty in there as well. Whatever the resonances, this is art.

And the final point to be made, as regards Duchamp and those of a similar artistic achievement who followed him, is that this kind of art makes very little sense at all in terms of aesthetics and the logic of beauty, however broad one's conception of it. If the aesthetics of 'beauty' were the only yardstick by which we could judge presentational material, then modern art would have to be counted as a dismal failure, and mostly quite meaningless. Modern art simply does not bear visual comparison with classical museum pieces, and would seem to be a ridiculous – even pathetic – attempt by modern artists to circumvent all the necessary hard work and exacting technical standards required for orthodox artworks. Many critics continue – even after a century – to interpret modern art in this light, seemingly unable to grasp that contemporary works might be operating on different principles, and attempting to achieve a wholly different outcome. But the moment one sees that modern art is narrative, and perspectival, and has nothing to do with classical beauty, then it begins to make sense as a substantial and worthwhile enterprise in its own right. Modern art speaks to our ability to connect to the minds of others, and to join with them in the worlds that they present, and in this it has a huge amount to say for itself.

Good and bad: successful and unsuccessful attempts at art

To the extent that we have established, objectively, what art is in itself, it follows that we ought now to be able to distinguish between that which is good art and that which is bad. This is because we can apply objective criteria to all aspects of art, independent of our own particular likes and dislikes, and simply judge whether an artist has managed to orchestrate a sufficiently strange and uncanny world through their artworks for that world to qualify as 'art'. It may not be a world that one particularly cares to explore, but that does not prevent one from acknowledging its substantiality and cogency as an artistic achievement.

The Dadaists gave us readymades and all manner of other sculptural provocations, and it might seem from this that any sort of flotsam would therefore immediately qualify as art, provided you could get someone to display it. But it's not the ability to startle or perplex which is the art; it's the ability to employ an artwork in the service of a subtle narrative of sorts, and the art is in the narrative, not in the sensual features of the object. Craftspeople who latch on to bits of junk and present it as 'artworks' may or may not be exteriorising an interesting inner perspective, though a certain amount of investigation on the part of the viewer will soon tell them whatever it is they need to know.

12

EXAMPLES OF ART- BACON, WARHOL, BEUYS

Francis Bacon (1909-1992)

Francis Bacon is probably the least problematic of our case studies in that most people interested in art are prepared to acknowledge the power of his paintings, even if they don't much like looking at them. He has become a key figure in modern art not only for his striking imagery, but also because he was something of a traditionalist, using oil paint and canvas, and working within the gallery system; on top of which some of his paintings had classical overtones, perhaps making it easier for critics and curators to argue his case within conventional circles. Yet it remains quite amazing, when you stop to think about it, that a painter of his ferocity and singularity managed to get anywhere at all, let alone to the top of the tree. It's as if Joel-Peter Witkin were considered the world's most sought-after photographer, not someone like Annie Leibovitz or Mario Testino.

Bacon is still subject to critical thinking which is underpinned by a combination of aesthetic confusion and orthodox aesthetic assessment. It reaches its most naked form in the declaration by Margaret Thatcher, who was reputed to have described Bacon as 'That man who paints those dreadful pictures'[29]; she meant of course 'aesthetically dreadful' and 'ugly subject matter', revealing her conventional understanding of how paintings were supposed to look. But applying orthodox aesthetics to Bacon's work is not restricted to outsiders; John Richardson – 'art connoisseur' and long-time friend of Bacon – wrote at length on Bacon's 'inability to draw'[30], arguing the case that Bacon's characteristic distortions were the result of a serious technical deficiency, and not a magnificent form of disclosure; so presumably if Bacon had been to art school and been properly educated, we'd have had another journeyman El Greco, or perhaps a Velazquez. Worse still, Bacon himself seems to have been deeply unsure of his own achievement, claiming 'Actually, I hate those popes because I think the Velazquez is such a superb image that it was silly of me to use it.'[31] This is a disheartening example of a major artist feeling the pressure of convention, and conceding to some kind of transcendental artistic authority.

Bacon's work being what it was, it is relatively straightforward, using our definitions, to identify the 'art' in what he did. Bacon painted images of strange, distorted creatures trapped in box-like confines, and these images are quite unlike anything else in conventional painting. They reveal a realm of their own, as if Bacon had access to a parallel universe, and was showing us what he had found. Bacon's 'art' – his 'narrative' – is his presentation to us of this other world, such that we can, by connecting with it imaginatively as it were, 'experience it', at least momentarily, and at least vicariously. Though of course the type of narrative in question here is not like a plot-driven story, sustained by a sequential series of events in a temporal arc; this is a much more impenetrable affair, where the 'narrative' – such as it is, and whatever it might hope to be – can come to a dead halt with the image alone, and can find itself unable to proceed. You know there is more to what you see than meets the eye, but you don't know what this could be, or how you might find it. You can turn to other Bacon paintings, hunting for clues, but they end up as impenetrable as one another. What could be more artistically fulfilling ?

---

[29] Widely quoted; see for example in the New York Times's Francis Bacon obituary, April 29th 1992.
[30] See John Richardson 'Bacon Agonistes', in the New York Review of Books, December 17, 2009.
[31] New York Review of Books, Ibid.

> Illustrations: Francis Bacon 'Figure in a Landscape' (1945) Tate Gallery, London; 'Study after Velázquez's Portrait of Pope Innocent X' (1953) Des Moines Art Center, Iowa; and many other similar examples.

As regards the quality and depth of the Bacon's art, there are some aspects worth pointing out here. Startling imagery does not, of its own, make for art; there has to be more to it; there also has to be what we have labelled as 'narrative depth', in the sense that the imagery draws you into something other than a momentary shock of horror, or shock of the unexpected, or shock of disgust. Bacon's images are shocking, but in a way that goes beyond horror and disgust because it also announces to the viewer the possibility of an uncanny experiential realm, though without indicating how this might be pursued. In other words, we are shown a door to another world, but not told how we might pass through it. And it is the presence of this additional unsettling dimension to Bacon's work which qualifies it as 'art', and which separates it from the work of other craftspeople – whatever their chosen medium – who, working with images of negativity, end up as mere purveyors of shock and horror.

But even if we accept that, according to our definition, Bacon is a quintessential example of an artist, combining traditional artistic methods to achieve strange and disturbing artworks, this does not mean that everything he did was successful, or that there aren't any difficulties and problems with his art as a whole. This in turn brings up interesting aspects relating to how we engage with art itself, and how we best 'consume' and absorb it. For a start, Bacon is probably best experienced in small doses, governed by the principle that, when it comes to extremes, less is always more, and more ends up delivering less. Lovers of loud music know that after the initial ecstatic rush, it is very difficult to sustain intense levels of volume without very careful consideration of the dynamics of sound, if a deadening sameness is not to set in and undermine the overall experience. Which means that Bacon retrospectives can be disappointing affairs if too much is on display at one time, and it is not given enough contrast; the intensity of the major Bacon images always results in overload. Bacon is at his ultimate best when nestling in the midst of innocent aesthetic craftings such as traditional portraits and still lives, as was the case at Tate Britain some years ago, when 'Figure in a landscape' (1945) was a startling contrast to the paintings around it.

Andy Warhol (1928-1987)

It might seem as if Andy Warhol, with his bright and simple imagery, would be the last artist to qualify as offering anything strange and disturbing, but this is not the case, and actually amounts to a surprising misreading of his art as a whole, and a failure to acknowledge some of the most interesting dimensions to his art hidden in the plainest of plain sight.

Pop Art – which Warhol played a major part in establishing – has come to be understood as the veneration of popular imagery of the sort to be found anywhere and everywhere in everyday media, like advertising logos and news photographs; and the Pop Art style – like Warhol silkscreen pastiches – has itself become a form of recognisable decoration, merging in with the imagery it imitates and reveres. Pop Art design style is bright, colourful, simple and repetitive, and in many ways is somewhat childlike and infantile, and may appear to represent the epitome of a rather innocent and vacuous optimism. Warhol described himself as a 'deeply superficial person'[32], and many critics and commentators took him at his word, deciding that Pop Art was as empty as it was claimed to be.

And though it is easy to be persuaded that the apparently irreducible simplicity of Pop Art imagery means that it can't possibly contain hidden depths, this is (deeply) mistaken. Warhol did more than simply create an instantly recognisable and immensely popular trademark style, he also presented us with an entire take on life; one that we could vicariously flirt with, and then inhabit, at least for a moment or two; and it is this presentational take on life which is where Warhol's real art is to be located, not in the aesthetic features of his artworks. Now while it is undeniably true that Warhol's artworks can be taken 'at face value', as it were, as bits of cultural ephemera writ large – they make perfect sense as examples of a generic and anonymous and easily imitable design style – they become much more interesting and intriguing as portals into the Warhol world: a distinctive theatrical realm of militant superficiality, drug-addled thinking, glitzy nihilism and camp posturing. The 'strange and disturbing' dimension to this world is its camp nihilism and affectless languor; something like the polar opposite of a conventional approach to the 'seriousness' and 'profundity' of life.

How can relentless superficiality be considered a hidden depth ? Because the Warhol world was more than just colourful prints of Mao, Coke and Marylin; there were also films, magazines, people, music and events. The 'Warhol world' was a living environment; an entire inhabitable landscape; and failure to be able to acknowledge this will result in a failure to appreciate how

---

[32] Widely quoted, eg Menzies (2012) but authoritative original source as yet uncertain.

the 'Warhol world' – as a very real presence – feeds back into the artworks in a way that transforms them from unitary examples of rather simplistic aesthetic achievement into – as it were – items of furniture, or decorative elements of an entire theatrical world, of which Warhol himself, as a theatrical persona, was very much a part, as were his friends and hangers-on[33].

This is not an easy concept to explain to someone who, perhaps influenced by different ideas, is thinking in a different direction. It involves a crucial perspective shift from seeing artworks as aesthetic ends-in-themselves, to seeing them as manifestations of a distinctive state of mind that we, as viewers, not only can join in, but also *ought* to try to join in, if we are to experience the art at its most encompassing. This is not about trying to define into existence something which really isn't there in the first place: this is about noticing that some artists – Warhol in particular, but equally Jeff Koons and Joseph Beuys – did more than present bits of craft for us to admire as best we can; they also managed, through the totality of their personalities and their behaviour and public utterances, to create distinctive 'theatrical presences' – that is to say, inhabitable worlds of their own – and insofar as we are able to recognise and discern and detect these very distinctive presences, we are able to realise that they play a more important part in infusing the artworks with meaning than the aesthetic features of the artworks are capable of doing on their own.

To illustrate this, we can return to the idea of decorating the rooms of a house in a certain distinctive style. This would be more than just having knick-knacks here and there; this is bringing together objects and furniture and colours in such a way as to create an environment recognisably itself, such that anyone entering into it would immediately connect with it as something akin to the manifestation of a 'state of mind', or better a 'state of being' – an environment within which someone lives. Now depending on the exact nature of the decoration and furnishing, it might be possible, for someone very familiar with that decorated environment, to see a colour or an object in a completely different context and find themselves instantly transported – in their imagination, as a fleeting thought – to the original decorated environment under discussion here. In normal circumstances, this would be an example of an accidental trigger; you just happen to see something which reminds you of something else; but in the case of an artist, they are deliberately orchestrating this triggering of associations by crafting their work in such a way as to make it as full of associative resonances as possible, so that as soon as you see the artwork you are instantly transported – subliminally, perhaps, without really thinking about it, but no less forcefully – into their own special and distinctive artistic world. And this capacity – or talent – to draw you into their world is the real 'art' of the modern artist; not the aesthetic features of individual objects. Looked at individually, Warhol's artworks are technically

---

[33] See, for example, Stephen Shore's 'Factory: Andy Warhol' (2016), and many others.

slapdash, shoddy and empty; but understood as portals to the Warhol world, they are as powerful and significant and fascinating as anything anywhere in all of art.

We need to stress that Warhol's persona was very much a part of his whole theatrical presentation. Perhaps he never intended it to be that way, and perhaps – if he had ever been confronted with the ideas of art we are presenting here – he might even have denied it was an essential part of the mix, but these factors are incidental to the finished product: it is perfectly legitimate to 'curate' – as defined earlier – the 'Warhol artistic experience' as a totality, to include the lives and behaviours of Warhol and his circle, as if his artworks and their wider associations were part of a single theatrical mix. And very much more to the point: to the extent that one sees Warhol's art as equivalent to Warhol's world, his art immediately delivers a richness and fascination which cannot be found in the mere aesthetics of his individual works, either singly or collectively.

Now the idea of the artist's persona as an essential component of their art is not true in every case; it very much depends on circumstance, and on the self-awareness of the artist in question. Francis Bacon, for example, despite being a heavy drinker and a connoisseur of rough trade, was a relatively ordinary person outside of his art; and knowing about his personal life adds very little to an appreciation of the extraordinary realms he uncovered in his paintings; and in fact it diminishes the works to attempt to decoded them or explain them away in quasi-psychoanalytic terms; just as it is absurd to try to explain Hendrix's music in terms of the electrical circuits required for his guitars. Some artists create worlds which, once actualised, are able to exist quite apart from their creators; others create worlds which would be meaningless without knowing about their creator's persona and without feeling the presence of this persona in the works themselves.

And when it comes to assessing an artist's persona, the concept of 'self-awareness' is of course extremely difficult to argue conclusively one way or another. Is the 'persona' an act, or is it real ? How does the artist intend us – as their audience – to view them ? Are they making a deliberate effort to portray themselves in a certain light ? How do we know ? These sorts of questions occur at the periphery of art criticism, and involve grasping – in effect intuiting – the entirety of an artist's persona, and then being able to distinguish between a theatrical effect, and something occurring naturally, of which the artist may only be partially aware, and not able to control and change to any significant degree.

Prior to the richness of material available on the internet, it would not have been easy to gain access to a rounded picture of an artist's persona, nor would it have been easy to arrive at a studied conclusion as to the levels of theatricality they were employing in their presentation of themselves. In the 1970s it was an open question as to whether Andy Warhol was acting the part of Andy Warhol[34], or if what we saw was all we were ever going to get. The situation was compounded by the fact that Warhol had an extraordinary talent for articulating, in memorable phrases, the essence of a kind of glib superficiality – a camp nonchalance – which, when you thought about it, always began to seem more profound than it did when you first heard it. Was he a deep thinker, or did he just say the first thing that came into his head ? Ultimately, it doesn't much matter, because what we have – if we watch hours of footage of Warhol in action, talking and explaining himself – is a very distinctive, recognisable, inimitable, and, by any standard, substantial persona; and it is this persona which, when grasped as the centre point of the Warhol world, unavoidably gives new meaning to his artworks in a way which effectively transcends whatever one might have thought of them previously. They change from being desultory bits of student homework to being instances of a fascinating take on life.

We can expand the concept of the importance of an artist's persona by discussing that of Jeff Koons. Like Warhol, Koons also projects an extraordinary superficiality, as if all of human culture were reduced to surface textures and vacuous ephemera; yet instead of this being somehow repellent and shameful, it becomes an endless source of fascination in itself. Koons is not merely pretending to be the spokesperson for a cultural banality, and playing a role which he can slough off at will: he is incarnating triviality and monstrous superficiality in a most magical way. There is nothing in what he says and does, or has said and has done, which puts the slightest distance between what we see, and what we think we see. So if Koons is an 'act', and having us all on, then it is one of those magnificent performances which defies criticism.

Koons contrasts well with someone like Damien Hirst, in that Hirst – in his artworks and in his personality – is noticeably 'normal' and 'ordinary' in his calculations, and this effectively prevents him from exploiting himself as part of his overall artistic presentation. He is simply not singular enough as a person to be a living artwork – and to turn himself into an ongoing performance – and thereby to lend his creations a narrative dimension which would transform them into objects with a very real meaning in a larger and more distinctive artistic landscape; Hirst's artworks, whatever their poetic resonances and despite their recognisability, still don't lead us into a peculiar and fascinating realm of their own; they are simply instances of a certain type of creative crafting. Koons, on the other hand, is spectacularly peculiar in his seamless, fascinating and relentless banality, and we can witness this in everything he says and does[35].

---

[34] See for example any of the many filmed interviews with Warhol from the 1970s.
[35] More on this aspect of Koons in the article Zaaiman (2019) 'Jeff Koons: A Certified Extra-Terrestrial'.

The concept of an 'artistic image' as an artificial persona

So far we have tried to portray the idea of an artist creating a world – that is to say, an imaginative, narrative realm that we as viewers can enter vicariously – by following a conceptual trail which involves a shift from focussing on the aesthetics of an artwork, to the possibility of a different perspective which involves artworks offering the viewer a portal into a distinctive 'strange and disturbing' experiential realm. Some people might find it difficult, and even uncalled-for, to make this readjustment, preferring instead to remain within the parameters of aesthetics, and to judge artworks entirely in terms of physical features. The idea of having to negotiate unseen, extra dimensions may seem to be unnecessary to the artistic requirements at hand, yet the concept of an imaginative and narrative context as an essential starting point is well known to the worlds of pop music and acting, and has been for decades. Actors and pop groups often deliberately cultivate what is technically known as an 'image', and this image may or may not coincide with their actual personalities, though it is the extent to which they are able to maintain their image which is a key feature in their perceived 'authenticity'.

Not all actors and pop groups go to extreme lengths over an image, and the image business is now streamlined to the point where merely situating oneself in a particular genre will of its own generate an image by association, and this can then be maintained with a few standard and routinized pronouncements. Some images are very flexible; 'jazz musician', for example, can stretch from the highly straight-laced and disciplined to the shambling and debauched; whereas 'death metal guitarist' tends to be narrowly tribal, especially as regards appearance, and a doom-laden moodiness. But the point about 'image' is that it directs the audience to a type of imaginative, narrative experience – or at least, to a readiness for a certain very specific type of experience – well in advance of any actual meaningful contact with the experience itself: image tells you how to manage your expectations, and how best to direct your imaginings.

'Image' and 'genre' can be dismissed as less important than the presentational experiences themselves, but what these categories do is acknowledge, in an indisputable way, the reality of the existence of a narrative, imaginative 'contextual realm' or 'contextual dimension' which lies well beyond any brute presentational facts – whether of acting, or music – and which, when properly orchestrated, can have an immense impact on the appreciation of the crafted works themselves: changing an image, or changing a genre, always involves having the audience change their perspective, and have them experience the crafted material in a radically different way. The material itself may remain 'physically' the same, but the experience of it is transformed by having the audience engage with different realms of their imagination.

How does all this relate to art ? What we are trying to explain here is that artists are sometimes – depending on an amalgam of complex factors such as their personality, their motivational determination, and their charisma – able to employ something akin to an 'image' in the service of their overall artistic presentation, and this 'artistic image' is much more powerful and substantial than a mere genre category of an 'image'. And to the extent that an artist is able to actualise and maintain a characteristic and distinctive image, this image is the true locus – meaning the true generative centre – of their art, and the most important experiential realm to be grasped if the art is truly to be understood at all. Finding ways to decode and interpret individual artworks is all very well, but if it is not done in a context where the wider experiential realm indicated by the artworks has been adequately grasped, then it is likely to be mistaken and irrelevant.

Joseph Beuys (1921-1986)

Francis Bacon's art was to be found in his artworks; the details of his personal life really don't add anything to the extraordinary experiential possibilities his paintings bear witness to; and in fact any attempt at psychoanalytic decoding demonstrates a complete misunderstanding of art itself, and most likely an inability to appreciate it in the first place. Warhol managed to shift the locus of his art from his artworks to a much wider and more fascinating 'lived world': an ongoing theatrical performance which included more or less all aspects of his life and the life of his close circle; and this theatricality then fed back into the artworks, granting them a new and more expansive meaning than they otherwise would have had.

Yet even if we disregard the Warholian world itself as the true locus of Warhol's art, we would still have had the 'Pop Art style', which owes much to Warhol's imagery. And this in turn means that, even by a trivial aesthetic definition of art as 'attractive shapes and colours', Warhol would still have a significant place in art history; not so Joseph Beuys, who, in common with many other key figures in modern art, simply cannot be adequately understood in traditional aesthetic terms.

Like Warhol, Beuys's art is properly to be located in himself, as a strange and distinctive performative persona. His sculptures, installations and graphic works derive almost all their meaning from being manifestations of the 'Beuys world' which, although given a certain measure of rational explanation by Beuys himself, can easily be seen as both mysterious, and impenetrable. Beuys had a fixation – 'obsession' doesn't quite capture it – with the substances 'felt' and 'fat', and he incorporated these materials into many of his densely baffling artworks, including the famous 'Fat Chair' (1964), 'Fat Corner' (1982), and 'Felt Suit' (1970). Beuys claimed that felt and fat were key elements used by Russian Tartars to restore him to health after an aircraft crash during WW2 – his near lifeless body was supposedly slathered in fat and wrapped in felt – but even if the story were true – and there is good reason to believe it is not – it doesn't make sense as a 'reason' to spend the next 40 years producing perplexing artworks made of felt and fat. The reasoning might have a certain momentary appeal to it, but it can't sustain itself against the facts. It's being asked to explain too much, and collapses into implausibility. And it is this kind of break in coherence which makes Beuys so interesting.

Beuys often gave reasoned and detailed accounts of what he was doing, and what his art meant. He was neither reclusive nor taciturn. His explanations included elements of environmentalism and political activism, and this made him seem very contemporary in the 1970s –at least to the student population in Europe – making him somewhat iconic, and certainly a figurehead for student-era mysticism; as if he were a shamanistic version of Noam Chomsky.

If we take Beuys and his theories seriously – meaning treating them as one would any philosophical account, and analysing their content systematically according to the laws of rational thought and coherence – we miss the point entirely. Beuys was an artist, and a performer, and he was presenting us with an open-ended theatrical narrative, centred on his own peculiar take on life. Knowingly or unknowingly, he had created a substantial theatrical pretence that was capable of sustaining and transforming almost any amount of content, physical or theoretical, without weakening the distinctiveness of his central conceit. He could, for example, find simple ways of turning almost any physical object into yet another distinctive 'sculptural' item in the Beuys landscape, and so incorporating it into his ongoing narrative performance.

The narrative begins with his peculiar appearance: the boots, the fisherman's vest, the Homburg hat, the haunted facial expression. Who is this man, we feel compelled to ask, and what can he tell us ? We want to hear the voice, and share his thoughts. And having captured our attention with his oddness, and having established this magnificently unsettling presence, he can hardly go wrong, artistically speaking. Truth and fiction, sense and nonsense, fat and felt; none of it really matters; it was now all about the performance, and of course Beuys had an instinctive talent for maintaining and expanding his mysterious portrayal of himself.

Naturally enough, this brings up a host of complex questions, about the curation and maintenance of art, some of which we have touched on previously. Beuys's art, like that of Jeff Koons and Andy Warhol, derives its power and meaning from the singularity and intensity of his persona; and though he created many unforgettable images, the artworks are almost incidental; this is not the case with Francis Bacon, whose art stands apart from his personality, and could easily exist without it. But if an artist establishes a powerful and luminous theatrical persona, do they curate themselves into an inescapable prison of their own making ? Can they break out of it ? Is it not possible to take the 'political' and 'ecological' Beuys seriously, and judge him according to the standards of ordinary discourse ? Theoretically yes, but like any other almost watertight persona, it would take a huge amount of time-consuming effort to overturn people's entrenched expectations, and this would be especially difficult in the case of an artist who has made 'otherness' and 'oddness' and 'peculiarity' an essential feature of their theatrical presentation.

Summary: three archetypical artists

Bacon, Warhol and Beuys represent three distinctive types of theatrical, narrative artistic possibility, stretching from art which stands on its own, to art which incorporates the artist into the mix. All three artists have presented art which reveals, when properly understood, strange and disturbing experiential opportunities.

Understanding Modern Art

13

EXAMPLES OF 'NOT ART' - EMIN & HIRST, POLLOCK, PICASSO

One of the most confusing and disheartening aspects of modern art – if and when you take a real interest in it – is that there seems to be no way to discriminate between one thing and another, and so no way to break out of the vicious – and tedious - circle of subjectivity. There doesn't seem to be any way of telling whether one artist is more deserving of your attention than another, and so we are immediately thrown back on our own likes and dislikes. The opinions of critics can help push sentiment in one direction or another, but the more you read art criticism, the more you realise the critics are no more in possession of decisive objective information than anyone in the street. Modern art just seems to be a complete free-for-all.

This is why it is important to be able to clarify the principles of art, such that they can be applied anywhere and everywhere, and such that they do not depend on one's personal likes and dislikes, and cannot be distorted by personal prejudice. The principles of art should be objective, and impartial, and analysable in cold intellectual terms, even though they would have to be applied to phenomena which call for imagination and emotion and experiential states of consciousness. There is nothing outrageous about this kind of proposition.

So having outlined how to understand three archetypical artists, we can now turn to archetypical craftspeople who, despite popular conceptions, don't qualify as authentic artists by our definition. This is not because they are not good at what they do – they clearly are good at it – but because 'what they do' doesn't, by our definition, rise to the standards of art. 'Creative crafting' it most certainly is, but as we have argued, creative crafting is not the same as art. For art to be art, it must not only have its own narrative content, this content must be characteristically and unavoidably 'strange and disturbing': it must reveal something we aren't already in possession of.

Tracey Emin (1963-) & Damien Hirst (1965-)

Both Emin and Hirst are famous for their sculptural work; an unmade bed and its immediate surroundings in the case of Emin, and various pickled animals in vitrines in the case of Hirst; although they both also produce drawings and paintings and installations, and other bits and pieces. And perhaps their greatest talent is their ability to remain newsworthy, and have collectors part with large sums of money for their work.

From an artistic point of view, the problem with both of them is that the narrative content of their work never discloses anything which could be described as strange and disturbing, or even particularly interesting. Their work only ever discloses ordinary ideas, with ordinary resonances, even in those instances which might be termed 'surprising', or 'unexpected' or 'unusual'. The gallery-going public might think that coming up with a pickled shark in a tank, or a soiled bed with condoms, is fascinating stuff, and well worth taking a look at, as well as being guaranteed of headlines; but the fascination, such as it is, rests firmly – perhaps even entirely – on its ability to maintain a startling contrast with standard museum pieces – that is to say, with oil paintings and classical sculptures – and once you have realised that that is the fullest extent of their impact, and that there is very little narrative content beyond the obvious, and almost nothing to connect with other than what is in front of you, the work rapidly loses its value. We've had all kinds of stuff in galleries before, from urinals, to shit in tins, to heads of frozen blood, to anything you can think of; and adding one or two more startling items to the list, without an interesting accompanying narrative, doesn't really advance any sort of disclosure, or reveal any realms of experience we are not already a party to. For art to be art, it has to take us somewhere we couldn't get to any other way. Showing us different angles on what we already know is the preserve of creative crafting, and of aesthetics, and of life in general, but not of art.

This is not about trying to denigrate or underplay the achievements of either Emin, or Hirst, or of any of the other very many successful artists worldwide who exhibit provocative objects in the hope of causing a stir. This kind of sensationalism is both popular and entertaining, and probably keeps the presentational crafting industry alive while we wait for real artists to come along. As has been said before, the point of 'art', as opposed to the point of 'aesthetics', is to disclose and reveal to us those realms of imaginative experience which allow us to confront – in a safe and vicarious way – the negative and unsettling aspects of life that in our ordinary day to day existence we would most certainly want to avoid. Art allows us to explore all aspects of 'negativity' from a distance – as abstractions and representations – so that we can savour and contemplate these things as if we were watching a play, or a film. If we only want reassurance, or comfort, we can turn instead to beautiful things, and enjoy their aesthetic features.

The distinction between the vicarious negativity offered by art and the comforting reassurance offered by aesthetic beauty is obviously never as clear cut as we might want it to be. We can't be sure when casually approaching an artist's work for the first time whether or not they are offering us access to something fascinating and uncanny, or something merely provocative and startling. Is a pickled shark in a see-through tank strange and disturbing ? It might be; but we need to know more. If Hirst only ever did pickled animals, and lived in a clearly constricted universe of preserved and embalmed items - with a distinctive public persona to match – our interest would clearly be aroused, but Hirst's artworks are all over the place, and whether it's opportunism or creative compulsion, his work somehow lacks coherence and authenticity.

> **Illustration: Damien Hirst 'The Physical Impossibility of Death in the Mind of Someone Living' (1991): the famous 'shark in the tank'.**

Yet how do we assess 'authenticity' in this instance ? Jeff Koons, for example, is every bit as market-orientated and opportunistic as Hirst, yet he radiates the values he encapsulates in his work. He seems to be exactly what he says he is, with no hint of a calculating hinterland; not so with Hirst, who just isn't able to generate the requisite persona. But would that it were that simple: Koons doesn't ever seem to be 'acting' in interviews, whereas Gilbert and George clearly are, yet Gilbert and George manage an act which is both fascinating and unsettling, and which certainly qualifies as artistic: it's all about being able to orchestrate a certain mysterious quality, which is sometimes there, and sometimes not. There are no hard and fast rules about exactly what to do to generate an uncanny sense of oddness, otherwise art would be altogether an easier proposition.

> **Illustration: any video on YouTube of a Gilbert and George interview will show clearly their weirdly symbiotic manner**

Tracey Emin's work also repays close analysis in the light of our definition of art. There are many people who feel compelled to question her artistic significance despite being unable to articulate exactly what they think is lacking in her work, given that she is hardly the first to put on display bits and pieces of homely detritus, and given that, if you're not really clear in your mind what art is anyway, exhibiting domestic junk may well contain some meaningful hidden narrative, perhaps known only to the professionals. But what is Emin's narrative ? Basically that of a troubled soul who is trying to exorcise some of her sexual and psychological demons by turning them into crafted objects of various kinds, from sculptures and installations, to wall hangings and confessional writings.

'Confessionalism' is of course a standard form of creative underpinning, with standard requirements: to keep the audience interested and amused, you have to introduce elements that people expect art to explore, whether it be sex, or violence, or criminality, or mental illness. Emin uses sexual titillation as a key enticement, teasing the audience with the promise of further outrage, while – sensibly perhaps – never quite delivering. She has also maintained a public persona as a drunken rabble-rouser and someone unafraid of lewd sexual utterances, though this has not prevented her from becoming a Royal Academician.

What Emin's artistry amounts to is a kind of quasi-medical roadshow, where she puts herself forward as a living case study – accompanied by crafted evidence – which she thinks is worthy of our attention. Where her work differs from the case studies psychology students have to familiarise themselves with is that, as crafted presentational material, it amounts to a form of entertainment, and not to a pedagogical device. But the real problem is not with her chosen contextualisation, it's with the rather straightforward fact that, when all else has been said and done, her work just isn't characteristically 'artistic', as we define it. It just isn't either strange or disturbing, or even particularly interesting. It's blunt, and self-obsessed, unimaginative, and dull; and if the whiff of sexual titillation were removed from the overall mix, there would be nothing to hold our attention at all. The unmade bed – her most famous piece by far – hints at something vaguely bodily, but we never get to see it, and in the end we're left struggling for the significance of a rather ordinary item of household furniture that looks like a lot of beds most people have seen at one time or another. Emin's work is often seriously anticlimactic.

> Illustration: Tracey Emin: 'My Bed' (1998);
> an installation, Tate, London

How then to account for her undeniable success ? We would have to say that she has found a way to orchestrate and exploit a perfectly ordinary and widespread interest many of us have in lewd female sexual behaviour, while somehow conferring on it the status of artistic respectability. We can study her crude drawings and semi-nude photographs in the secure knowledge that it is 'art', as opposed to merely grim voyeurism. But in terms of the intensity of her offering, Emin compares badly with, say, Annie Sprinkle or Lydia Lunch, or even Sarah Lucas who, with a fraction of the output, still comes across as infinitely more substantial.

Jackson Pollock (1912-1956), and 'Abstract Art' in general

We have chosen Pollock to represent Abstract Art not only because is he the most famous example of that genre, but also because his work is distinctively recognisable, and so would seem to lend itself to all kinds of meaningful interpretations. The essence of Abstract Art is of course that it is non-narrative, and relies entirely on colours and shapes for its effect, though this is not seen as problematic for those who are open to art mysticism.

Art mysticism is all about using crafted material to spark off, or encourage, or generate, imaginative resonances, and these resonances are then used to bathe the viewer in various feelings and sensual states of mind, leading to somewhat altered forms of consciousness, akin, though less intense and consuming, to religious mystical experiences. And the whole point of classical art – as we have now come to understand it in the 21st century – is to arouse in the viewer subtle experiential states of mind of an aesthetic nature, centred on ideas of beauty and sublime attractiveness, and so have the viewer think that these experiences are highly refined and cultured and worthy, over and above being merely pleasurable.

And of course being able to enter into semi-mystical states of mind is essential to understanding the appeal of Abstract Art, even if no one ever puts it in such bold terms. Though of course we have to acknowledge that there are important rules to this process, and they cannot be ignored, even when dependent on what might look like very trivial distinctions. For example, any child can, with minimal guidance, produce a Pollock drip painting, but a child's version never becomes a Pollock, and so never arouses semi-mystical states of mind, principally because it is not situated in a context which would knowingly and willingly be prepared to endorse its crafterly value. Yet the value in question is not some tangible asset – because the tangible elements in both cases are indistinguishable drips on canvas – it is the consensual agreement of the parties that go to make up the endorsement itself. In other words, if we can get a group of people to agree that one group of squiggles on a canvas are somehow 'meaningful', and that yet another identical group of squiggles are somehow 'not meaningful', then the rest will follow: academics and critics can substantiate the situation with complex arguments, and the artworld can authorise and monetise the chosen object, while utterly rejecting its identical twin.

Does this mean that Abstract Art is the Emperor's New Clothes ? Not exactly; we are dealing here with realms of human experience where faith and imaginings and desires swirl around without any decisive grounding, and where people are able to make decisions on the basis of deeply-held feelings and intuitions, and intellectualise their choices later. For very many people, art is a playground of imaginative resonances, and given that art appreciation remains an arcane and specialised pursuit, there is no pressure on anyone to clarify their thoughts about art, or work out a consistent set of objective principles. Like religion, art encourages theoretical system building on the basis of a few self-validating feelings and perceptions.

Having said all this, it doesn't make sense to attempt to assess Pollock on the basis of a conceptual trail through art history and the theoretical principles of Abstract Art. It is enough to say that all Pollock really achieved was to produce large-scale decorative canvases, of the sort which could humanise the foyer of an office building. These canvases are singular enough to be recognisable by those with a basic art education, but they are completely devoid of narrative content, and so can't, singly or collectively, offer us a portal to any sort of experiential realm, other than that of aesthetic sensation. They don't point to anything other than a new form of possible decorative feature – that is to say, a feature framed and limited to a particular fixed space – because an entire house of Pollock-like decorative wallpaper would be an unimaginable nightmare.

All the major Abstract artists suffer from a crucial narrative deficiency, which means that Abstract Art is never more than shapes and colours on a surface, sometimes done prettily, sometimes not. If the shapes and colours appeal to you, then well and good, but they have nothing else to offer besides themselves. Despite mountains of theoretical verbiage in their defence[36], they have no story to tell, no experiential realm to reveal. Some Abstract artists developed distinctive and easily-identifiable styles – Franz Kline, Rothko, Mondrian, Barnett Newman – but this hardly confers extra significance on their shapes and colours, or makes them less essentially decorative. Abstract Art is not 'art' – it's aesthetic creative crafting.

> **Illustrations: the singular works of Robert Ryman (1930-2019); master of 'monochrome abstract conceptualism.'**

Is that the end of the matter ? Can we say conclusively that abstraction is non-narrative ? Once again, not exactly. Robert Ryman (1930-2019), for example, with his peculiar obsession with canvases of white and almost white paint, can be considered an artist of the first order. His monomaniacal fixation takes us beyond decorative colours and shapes into a claustrophobic realm of non-decorative colourlessness and shapelessness. It's apparently abstract on the surface, but of such an extreme nature as to have become paradoxically narrative again, though this time of a most bizarre order, right on the edge of sense and nonsense, sanity and insanity, hope and despair. But this all means that, improbable though it may sound, it is possible to orchestrate abstraction in the service of narrative; Rachel Whiteread (1963-) has shown in her sculptural work that what is ordinarily dismissed as inconsequential space can be solidified and transformed into uncanny and magical presences with a life of their own. Art is such that even when you have identified its principles, and are able to detect its distinctive realm of narrative, you have no idea where you might find it.

> **Illustrations: the sculptural works of Rachel Whiteread (1963-)**

Pablo Picasso (1881-1973)

For most people Picasso represents, in every respect, the archetypical artist, so trying to argue as we are doing here that he somehow does not qualify as an artist seems almost completely absurd, and a self-inflicted and fatal blow

---

[36] Clement Greenberg again; see the bibliography, especially 'Collected Essays and Criticism' (1995).

to our entire theory. But as we have said before, unless we can hold fast to a clear distinction between aesthetics – as the realm of beauty – and art – as the realm of a distinctive realm of narrative – then we can never move towards establishing objective criteria in our understanding of 'art'.

No one would attempt to deny the utterly extraordinary creative talent that characterised Picasso's work throughout his life, nor would we even attempt to diminish this in some interpretative way. All that he achieved, in terms of stylistic innovation and sheer creative genius, stands exactly as it is, but what we are trying to clarify is the precise nature of his achievement, and the limits of its reach. There is something so flagrantly confident about almost all his work that it seems to validate itself collectively and defy radical criticism; yet at the same time, despite its many radical innovations, it still manages to locate itself firmly in the classical tradition.

In fact, Picasso makes most sense when understood in terms of classicism; it's as if he had dedicated himself solely to testing, by employing various stylistic innovations, the limits of classical compositional principles, to see what the outcomes would be. There is very little narrative in his works, the major tension being towards distortion and abstraction, though these elements are always in the service of aesthetics, rather than of experiential disclosure. So rather than reveal to us strange new realms, he shows us how distorting features of the familiar can still be considered 'attractive' and 'interesting'.

The Picasso persona doesn't seem to have much of a narrative either. Beyond a certain requisite Bohemianism – mainly womanising – he seems to have been quite dull, and the only thing interesting about him was his irrepressible aesthetic gift. We are not trying to overturn what has been said earlier and argue now that you need to incarnate your art in your life, yet there is no sense that behind the sensuality of his work Picasso was trying to show us something other than what we can already see. Picasso did not possess a hidden hinterland; he was exactly the person he appeared to be.

The close association between the idea of 'art' – meaning creative crafting – and the idea of 'Picasso as the quintessential artist' is likely to remain strong - and probably even last forever - as most people are not much interested in the presentational possibilities beyond captivating imagery, and so are perfectly happy to stick with the idea of vibrant colours and swirly shapes as 'art'. But if presentational work is to 'tell' you something, if it's to disclose imaginative possibilities over and above immediate sensual beauty, and lead you into imaginative congruence with new perspectives, then it will employ narrative elements which are not restricted to beauty and attractiveness. And in this way of clarifying the principles of crafting, Picasso is not strictly speaking an artist, he is basically a creative craftsman.

14

UNDERSTANDING ART - FURTHER CONSIDERATIONS

We will assume at this stage that our elemental distinction between aesthetics – crafted presentational material – and art – narrative presentational material – has by this stage (finally !) been grasped and understood, and that we can now move on to a direct appreciation – in the light of our definition and understanding - of some of the wider characteristics of art itself. The idea here is to deepen our understanding of art by bringing into focus some of the elements of our experience of it.

When we decide that an item of presentational material is 'intriguing', what might we mean by this ? 'Intriguing' is one of the most basic labels we could apply to something we are looking at, or listening to, and if we're not simply being polite, 'intriguing' means that the object of our attention promises more than can be comprehended, or appreciated, in a single moment, or even a single viewing; and that, if we give it time, it will continue to enthral, and continue to inform us of something we don't already know. In other words, it will continue to 'disclose' something valuable to us over time, the 'something' being an essential element of its particular nature.

'Disclosure' – the ability of a presentational object to tell us something intriguing and beguiling – is a key concept in our understanding of art, because it identifies exactly what it is about art that art can do, as opposed to merely decorate and prettify our environment. Art can also disclose beauty, and skilful technique, but this type of aesthetic information is of a different order from that of narrative and perspectival congruence, which essentially involves our joining the artist in the world that they have disclosed to us, and then following – as best we can, depending on our imaginative capacities – the ideas and resonances that it delivers to us.

So art needs to be intriguing and beguiling, rather than beautiful, if it is to fulfil its own distinctive purpose. And to be intriguing, it has to show us realms of experience with which we are not ordinarily familiar, and these realms can be characterised, somewhat clumsily, as 'strange and disturbing', combining ideas of the uncanny, the unusual, the unsettling, the fascinating, the enthralling, and so on.

Art just isn't that easy to create

Now if the idea of 'art' presented here has been somewhat difficult to grasp in one go - depending as it does on grasping several sets of crucial distinctions, -it is just as difficult to create. This is part of the reason why most craftspeople remain 'creative craftspeople' instead of becoming artists, as it is easier to produce objects which have 'aesthetic interest' than artworks which have 'artistic interest'.

Because how, exactly, do you establish a context in which the 'strange and disturbing' can manifest itself ? This question is itself difficult to formulate in a way that begins to point towards an answer, because the whole idea of a 'strange and disturbing' element to an artwork requires the ability to grasp an ethereal 'aura' which is both elemental and foundational, yet which may appear either subtle or invisible to those whose thoughts and sensitivities are differently calibrated, or who are simply looking for different qualities in an artwork. How do you redirect their perceptions ? How do you tell someone to 'forget the aesthetics' and concentrate instead on the 'take' behind and underneath the art object ? More importantly, from a creative perspective, how do you orchestrate the elements of the medium you are using such that they will project the weird and wonderful ? Can 'weirdness' be something you can deliberately bring under control and then manipulate ?

This question brings us back to the complexities of identifying the precise moment – or the precise stage in time – when something changes from being a mere piece of crafted presentational material into a work of art. Did Andy Warhol set out to be the kind of artist we have characterised him as ? Most likely not; he simply did what he liked doing, and the weird and wonderful 'Warhol world' simply came into being over time – of its own accord – imperceptibly, perhaps, if you were a witness to Warhol's activities in the early part of his career, but easy enough for us to identify with hindsight.

'Incorrect' as a (musical) genre

In order better to understand the kind of mental congruence required to grasp 'art' as we define it, we will outline the concept of 'Incorrect' or 'Outsider' art, especially as it applies to music.

This from rateyourmusic.com:

> Outsider musicians are often termed "bad" or "inept" by listeners who judge them by the standards of mainstream popular music. Yet despite dodgy rhythms and a lack of conventional tunefulness, these often self-taught artists radiate an abundance of earnestness and passion. And believe it or not, they're worth listening to, often outmatching all contenders for inventiveness and originality...
>
> Anybody trying to be strange is not an outsider. Classic outsider music artists include--don't worry if these are unfamiliar names--The Shaggs, Florence Foster Jenkins, Jandek, Shooby Taylor, Wesley Willis, Brute Force, Ya Ho Wha 13/Father Yod, Little Marcy, song-poem singers, T. Valentine, Lucia Pamela, Fran Baskerville the Singing Psychic, Peter Grudzien, Arcesia, Anton Maiden, certain school bands, some street musicians and a host of others few people have ever heard. And of course the list of celebs inadvisedly essaying songs includes William Shatner, Jack Webb, Telly Savalas, Leonard Nimoy, Joey Bishop, Xaviera Hollander, Ed McMahon, Sebastian Cabot and even opera great José Carreras who did some stupefying Christmas recordings.
>
> Like Portuguese and Spanish explorers, Irwin Chusid has made the first maps of outsider music in his book Songs in the Key of Z[37] and in a radio show co-hosted by Michelle Boulé called Incorrect Music. Some outsider recordings have been released by Arf! Arf! Records and others but much tends to be found in more circuitous routes. Many links are on the Incorrect Music site.

---

[37] Chusid (2000).

Outsider Music is NOT:
- novelty recordings
- merely bad music
- avant-garde weirdness
- exotica/lounge music unless it's really inept or genuine but strange
- outdated musical conventions (mainstream in the 1920s, campy now)
- anything where the artist is conscious or aware of being "bad" or "kitschy"; - it can't be deliberate

Outsider Music IS (or can be):
- inept but sincere
- celebrity vocals (aka "Golden Throats")
- incredibly pretentious
- the work of people with, er, problems
- like eavesdropping
- stuff that makes you go "What the heck?!"

Chusid himself stated that the key element to 'Incorrect' music was a genuine 'lack of self-awareness', meaning that the artiste is unaware of the distance between their understanding of an artistic standard, and the commonly accepted standard itself; leading, effectively, to crafted material which is unintentionally unusual and peculiar, and therefore characteristically singular. For this type of music to be worth listening to, it must obviously have interesting qualities over and above its singularity, but the point about 'Incorrect' is that, for it to exist as a genre at all, we have to be able to acknowledge differing levels of artistic 'awareness', centred around something like an accepted norm. This doesn't have to involve being patronising (or condescending) to those who fail to achieve the norm; it's more about enjoying creativity which, in its distinctive distance from the consensus, discloses to us something beguiling and intriguing; and in this way Outsider Art is more likely to be more elementally fascinating and unsettling than art crafted in accordance with more conventional ideas.

And in order to be able to understand the concept of 'Incorrect', you also have to be able to appreciate that an artist's 'intention' – that is to say, what they might have deliberately intended and hoped their artwork would say – really has only something of an accidental or tangential relationship with the finished product; and although it would be wrong to ignore an expressed intention entirely, it is only ever one element in an artwork, and not necessarily the most important one. As was discussed in an earlier section, 'curation' is key to situating art in an appropriate presentational context, and it takes precedence over all other forms on intentionality, including an artist's beliefs. And paradoxically, one of the preconditions of qualifying for Incorrect is that the artist is not allowed to conceive of their work as 'art' – that is, as irony or satire – as it has to be unambiguously sincere.

Returning now to the theme of the difficulties inherent in creating art, we can see that at least part of the problem lies with the exacting standards our definition entails. It's not that we have deliberately set out to create an exclusive and elitist conception, but rather that, when we have cleared away all that is not-art, we are left with a distinctive presentational realm which mysteriously entails more than merely deciding to craft 'in a certain way', in the confidence that the outcome will be 'art'. And because art is more than mere craft, and more than mere crafterly skill and talent, it cannot be forced into existence by willpower alone: it is orchestration of subtle forces which are not at the disposal of just anyone at any time.

The point about art is that it should disclose something intriguing to the viewer, not just appeal to their aesthetic sensitivities. 'Intriguing' means opening up imaginative realms with which we are not routinely familiar, and in so doing disclosing something to us that we could not reach – vicariously - any other way, because, as has been stated earlier, 'art' is a form of abstraction, at least one step removed from 'real life'.

Activism and Political Art

Now to the extent that we can bypass the distractions and grasp art where it is most crucially located – in a narrative, imaginative realm – we can also understand how easily a poor grasp of art can tempt artists – and viewers – into engaging with all manner of lesser presentations in the belief that these are where the real power of art lies. And perhaps the most tempting of these is the idea of making some sort of political or social statement, and grabbing people's attention through a kind of immediacy and relevance. This then has the art mystical consequence of making the artist and their artworks feel contemporary and valuable, even at the risk of condemning themselves to immediate obsolescence. Though art being art, this is never a certainty, and it is always possible that the most specific and time-bound crafting turns out to be the most resonant and enduring, but we know from political art of the Weimar period and Nazi Germany that what may have been powerful at the time can quickly become stale and empty once circumstances change and the moment of relevance has passed. One has only to think of the 'anti-Vietnam' war posters of the late 1960s to see how quickly activism becomes dated.

Illustrations: anti-Vietnam war posters of the 1960s & 1970s.

15

GALLERY GOING- ENGAGING WITH ART & "CONSUMING" IT

Understanding 'art' as 'narrative disclosure' has enormous implications for our engagement with art, at all levels. Art is then no longer concerned with aesthetic mysticism, and swooning at beauty, but is instead about something much more imaginative and immersive, as well as being subtler. Art is about connecting with the worlds revealed through artworks, and then exploring their possibilities.

This does not involve preventing and negating the ideas of those who want to reduce all art to aesthetics, but it does involve – for those looking for something deeper and more interesting - heading in an entirely different experiential direction. It involves approaching the features of an artist's work from a different perspective, and bypassing much of what most people think is the 'proper' way of appreciating art. The art of Gilbert and George is not about standing in front of their gigantic posters and trying to squeeze relevance and meaning out of them; it is about connecting with their strange perspective on life, and taking it on, and exploring it – intuitively - as far as you can. It is about trying to imagine the world from their point of view, and directing your perceptions through their perceptual template, even if, as may well be the case, their perspective is a wholly theatrical construct, and not a reality. Jeff Koons, Andy Warhol and all the rest of them may well be having us on, and pretending to ideas and perspectives that don't really exist, but who cares ? It's not the point. What's important is that they've given us imaginative worlds to immerse ourselves in, and whether or not they actually represent a locatable and objective reality is neither here nor there.

Art criticism

As things stand, art criticism (of contemporary art) is almost entirely about deconstructing the specific features of individual artworks and then offering suggestions as to how they may be interpreted. And these deconstructions nestle in anecdotal and biographical detail, the more salacious the better, so as to make the review interesting. These are standard methods of making any news article 'read well', and as such can hardly be faulted. But the point is that they only represent a narrow aesthetic understanding of art, and so never really get to grips with art as a form of narrative disclosure. We can see for ourselves the aesthetic features of a Bacon 'Pope', though perhaps not with the highly trained eye of the professional, and so may well be missing some of the finer aesthetic detail; but being led through a close reading of these features will not tell us anything at all about the experiential realm that this Pope reveals to us; and in fact it will misdirect us into thinking that having a command of aesthetic minutiae somehow serves as a full and complete appreciation of the painting itself, when this is the exact opposite of the case. Aesthetic detail is only ever subservient to the narrative of the painting itself, and the narrative has to be grasped in its own special way, as a portal to its own distinctive realm, not as a collection of crafterly details.

Now because most art criticism is confused as to where the 'art of art' actually lies, and therefore has to rely on aesthetic detail for interpretation, we can then understand the startling fact that most major art studies have very little to do with art 'in itself', and usually rely primarily on cultural history for their substance. So instead of shedding light on the experiential realm an artist has revealed to us, the critic will explain the art in terms of its cultural significance, and how it relates to other elements in a broader cultural context, whether historical or contemporary. A famous example is Robert Hughes's

'The Shock of the New'[38] television series from 1980, in which Hughes, under the guise of an exploration of modern art, was in fact presenting us with a study of a relationship between advances in modern technology and the effects of these advances on modern society; and using famous modern artworks as illustrative markers of this unfolding process. It was as if the artworks had no particular significance of their own, and only gained meaning as a manifestation of something else – in this case, a cultural shift of some kind – and so you could make an entire series about modern art without really dealing with the art in itself at all.

> **Illustration: the TV series 'The Shock of the New' (1980) by Robert Hughes; 8 episodes and a 2004 update 'The New Shock of the New', episodes available on YouTube and as DVDs.**

Dada – as an art movement – is a case in point. The art of Dada is to be located in a certain perspective, combining spontaneity and irrationalism and cultural nihilism; and if you want to grasp Dada you have to try, somehow, to take on the Dada mindset, and inhabit it. This is not an unreasonable or impossible request: we take on differing mindsets all the time, every day, if only momentarily and unconsciously. For example, if we are shown a photograph of a mass murderer, we might try to imagine, from the merest hints in their image, what it would be like to be them, and what it might be like to do the things that they have done, even if we are then repulsed by our own imaginings. This does not turn us into mass murderers; it is an automatic reflex in our imaginations, and an unavoidable attempt at meaningful congruence with the experience of others. Inhabiting the mind of a criminal is, for most people, an unpleasant occurrence, and we turn away from exploring it at any length; but this is where art comes in, because art, as a presentational opportunity for vicarious imaginings, offers us the contemplation of all kinds of unusual and disturbing experiences at a safe remove: art is implicitly a form of theatre, and a form of playacting, a form of make-believe.

So to 'explain' Dada, and interpret it appropriately - on its own terms, and not reducing it to something else - it is not enough to locate it historically or to describe how people responded to it; we want some ideas as to how best

---

[38] Television series, and accompanying book in various editions, eg Hughes (2013).

to inhabit it, and what it might be like to experience a Dadaist perspective from within. This is obviously much more difficult to articulate than simply describing the details of Dadaist artworks, or repeating gossip about various Dada artists' behaviour, or expressing opinions about one's aesthetic likes and dislikes, which is why most art criticism is not in fact about art at all, but rather about how art relates to other aspects of life and culture.

And to see this in action, it is worth browsing any recent art review in a major publication or website, and then judging how much or little of the text is to do with the art itself, and how much is 'extraneous material' designed only to entertain. Of course it could be argued that this is true of any type of popular journalism, but it means that no matter how many 'art reviews' you read, you're never really getting any closer – even by osmosis - to a meaningful understanding of art itself. Art criticism is almost always a form of misdirection.

Critical 'interpretative layering'

As was mentioned in an earlier section, the most popular way modern art has been interpreted has been to see modern artworks as representing, as it were, 'interesting ideas' made flesh, with the implication being that to appreciate modern artworks, you need to grasp the 'interesting ideas' they represent, and this basically involves a process of 'decoding' and 'decrypting'. There are many books now published on how to go about decoding and deconstructing modern art[39], and they all subscribe to the idea that artworks are like crossword puzzles, and that the art experience – in its totality - is more or less coextensive with an 'aha !' moment of clue resolution.

This reduces creative crafting to a very trivial affair, and turns the whole enterprise of art into a kind of magazine puzzle by other means. But even if we dismiss this approach to art as deeply misguided, it still brings to light a feature of the relationship between 'art theory' – as casually encountered – and the direct experience of art itself; and this is worth analysing in some detail. In other words, there is an important relationship

---

[39] See for example, Heller (2002); Acton (2010); and Ward (2018); or for heavyweight impenetrability, Bann (1991).

between the kind of information we inadvertently pick up about art, and the way we generally go about interpreting what we see or hear; and this relationship is of interest to both aesthetics and to a grasp of art proper.

Presentational material has no direct worldly utilitarian function, and so it takes us away from a physical, practical connection with the lived world and moves us instead into the realm of ideation and cerebral sensitivity. And for the intellect to have something to grasp, and to hold up for intellectual inspection, our ideas have to become abstracted and put into objective imagery of one kind or another, and the most useful and accessible of these abstractions are of course 'verbal descriptions'. These descriptive markers (keywords and phrases) give our experiences coherence and intersubjective currency, in that we can use them to communicate to others what we are thinking, and so are able to objectivise our thoughts in ways that help us grasp – and reflect on – our own thoughts as much as convey them to other people.

What we are saying is that experiencing crafted presentational material, whether strictly aesthetic or artistic, in the raw, without some kind of intellectual mediation, tends to be confused and confusing, swirling all over the place, and it only really comes together coherently when we find ways of putting it into words, followed by some kind of conceptual organisation. And to the extent that we are intellectually poorly informed, or haven't bothered to think things through, our conceptual organisation will be weak and unhelpful, confusing us as much as assisting us. And if such confusion becomes chronic, we tend to lapse into a kind of easy-going everyday mysticism, in which we draw strength from a 'who cares ?' and a 'so what ?' type of self-justification.

But if we genuinely enjoy experiencing art objects and art forms - even if we have no real idea what they are supposed to be all about - we will be inclined to latch on to words, phrases and descriptions we have come across that we believe articulate our experiences, even if these descriptions are misjudged and inappropriate to the experiences themselves. This is why there is such a market for art criticism and art interpretation in all its forms -from gallery tours to media reviews - testifying to the fact that anyone who seems to be able to help us articulate our vague and elusive encounters with art can be sure of an appreciative audience.

In its most basic form, everyday art theory – of the sort that we can pick up and apply to what we see and hear – amounts to what can be termed 'interpretative layering'. In other words, we gather together various ideas about an art object, and we find ourselves reminded of them when we encounter the object in a certain way, and this gives us a sense that we are somehow 'getting into' the 'inner meaning' of the artwork itself. We recognise that some ideas are somewhat superficial, and some are more penetrating, and in this way we subliminally rank interpretative ideas into vague layers of interpretative meaning, which we can reach for as and when the mood takes us. And if we hear or read of a new set of interpretative ideas, we can add those to our already existing mix, depending on how deeply we want to go into the subject.

But if we look at these interpretative ideas more closely, we can see that they have the paradoxical effect of substituting themselves for the experience of the actual artwork itself, so that what we end up experiencing is not the artwork directly, but rather ideas about it, some of which may have little or nothing to do with the art itself. This is rather like 'reading about music' instead of 'listening to it', and then coming to believe that 'reading about it' is in fact how you experience music itself.

We can try to illustrate this strange phenomenon by showing it at its most extreme, as it appears in scholarly studies. It can be most clearly and starkly illustrated through examples of 'close reading', whereby a heavily interpretative template is imposed on an art object, in the belief that this is what will constitute a meaningful encounter with that object; and the object is then subject to a detailed analysis, the idea being that, somewhere in all the ensuing deconstructive complexity, the 'art' of the object is slowly being brought to light.

Read, for example, Rosalind Krauss on Cindy Sherman:

> From the very outset of her project, in Untitled Film Still #2 (1977), she sets up the sign of the unseen intruder. A young girl draped in a towel stands before her bathroom mirror, touching her shoulder and following her own gesture in its reflected image. A doorjamb to the left of the frame places the "viewer" outside this room. But what is far more significant is that this viewer is constructed as a hidden watcher by means of the signifier that reads as graininess, a diffusion of the image that constructs the signified /distance/, a severing of the psychic space of the watcher from that of the watched.

> Illustration: Cindy Sherman:
> Untitled Film Still #2 (1977)

In Untitled Film Still #39 (1979), it is not so much the grain of the emulsion that establishes the voyeuristic remove, with its sense that one is stealing up on the woman, as it is a kind of nimbus that washes around the frame of the image, repeating in the register of light the sense of barrier that the door frame constructs in the world of physical objects.

> Illustration: Cindy Sherman:
> Untitled Film Still #39 (1979)

But in Untitled Film Still #81 (1979) there is a remarkably sharp depth of field, so that such /distance/ is gone, despite the fact that doorways are once again an obtrusive part of the image, implying that the viewer is gazing at the woman from outside the space she physically occupies. As in the other cases, the woman appears to be in a bathroom and once again she is scantily dressed, wearing only a thin nightgown. Yet the continuity established by the focal length of the lens creates an unimpeachable sense that her look at herself in the mirror reaches past her reflection to include the viewer as well. Which is to say that as opposed to the idea of /distance/, there is here the signified /connection/, and what is further cut out as the signified at the level of narrative is a woman chatting to someone (perhaps another woman) in the room outside her bathroom as she is preparing for bed.

The narrative impact of these images tends to submerge the elements through which it is constructed, elements such as depth-of-field, grain, light, etc. which, it would seem, are too easy to dismiss as merely "formal" integers, whereas they function as signifiers crucial to the semantic effect.[40]

> **Illustration: Cindy Sherman:**
> **Untitled Film Still #81 (1979)**

The kind of heavy intellectualisation that Krauss is demonstrating here is based on the assumption that Sherman's photographs – and other work like it – not only deserve close reading but that they also begin to disclose their secrets in ways that more straightforward and ordinary responses would miss. In other words, very close reading is the kind of decoding appropriate to understanding artistic photography; and along the way it also accords the study of modern art a substantiality it might otherwise lack, because it shows that if you put sufficient effort into your decoding, you will be rewarded with extra meaning.

The problem with this is that, unless the level of intellectualisation can deliver hidden information of an equivalent complexity and value – and hidden in plain sight, because what we are looking at is right in front of us – the decoding just ends up sounding very like hot air indeed. Anybody can describe a photograph of a cup of filter coffee in an American diner as a 'damning condemnation of effete western society', but this sort of interpretative overloading sounds pretentious and silly, and is a sure sign that people have lost their footing, if they had one in the first place.

More to the point in the case of Cindy Sherman, her 'art' is not located in the meanings to be found in, or extracted from, individual artworks, her art is all about her extraordinary solipsism, and her attempts to both celebrate and perhaps overcome this self-obsession by concentrating entirely on it, and then representing herself – as her only model – in an ongoing variety of different ways. The differences in each photograph and groups of themed photographs is always offset by a claustrophobic sameness, and while there is absolutely no law against close readings of the incidental detail in each artwork, in Sherman's case it completely obscures the central idea. To 'get' the art, you have to be able to lock into Sherman's mindset, at least that part of it which expresses itself in her photographs, and share with her her particular

---

[40] Krauss (2001) p.118 ff.

and distinctive quest to resolve the irresolvable contradiction between 'always different, always the same'.

'Gallery-going'

If one wants to elevate gallery going from a somewhat disconnected and disengaged ramble about decorated spaces, to something altogether more purposive and insightful, it becomes important to know what you are looking for. One has to undergo a shift from aesthetic passivity in which one expects an artwork to work its magic on you without you having to do anything yourself, to an active engagement where you seek clues as to whether an artist is able to disclose an interesting realm to you, or is simply presenting something in the hope that it will elicit a response. This will certainly involve reading around a subject, and watching videos, and testing one's ideas against the evidence, as well as developing a feel for the way the artworks themselves are able to act as portals to the 'art' which underpins them and gives them meaning. The approach here is quite different from that of the aesthetician, who – like a gourmet - relies on a sensibility which has been educated and refined over time, and which they trust to deliver the correct sensual judgement when confronted with aesthetic information. In fact, it is useful to think of traditional aestheticians – critics like Robert Hughes and Brian Sewell – as essentially 'gourmets of the visual'; people who delight in refining their visual sensitivity to the furthest degree.

The painter Chris Orr has put the case for aesthetic judgement in the clearest possible terms:

> So what is good and bad in Art, and how do the judges choose one picture as opposed to another? In the selection process the works come at you thick and fast brought in by a team of art handlers. You must make an instant decision. This has to be intuitive. Like going to a very large party you quickly work out who you want to talk to. There are second thoughts, for and against, but no time to do research or look for corroborating evidence. You have to trust your judgement built over years of looking. I remember the shock when I first went to Art School and was told that there was no progress in Art and that the definition of the bad in Art had changed many

times. This is the last bastion of an unreasonable world where intuitive feeling trumps all the myriad orthodoxies.

The net result is a contradictory exhibition, but this contradiction is at the heart of creativity. No open submission exhibition makes sense. It is the very surprising unpredictability that makes it both significant and entertaining. Walking into a display like this often leads to a kind of 'snow blindness'. The result of a large number of small scale, but intense images can put you into a bit of a spin, but look carefully dear viewer, and you will surely find something of great significance, even life changing for you. That is why I have chosen what I have chosen.

We can see how far Orr's view is from an art of narrative congruence, where you pick up on the realm being disclosed to you, and begin to explore it. Aesthetic art is about negotiating imagery of one kind or another, whether visual, or auditory, or tactile, or imaginary, as is the case with novels and poems, and letting the imagery capture you and alert you to the individual aesthetic features. Interestingly, Orr claims to be a fan of 'narrative':

I like pictures that tell a story. As well as the stories of life around us, the source may be an anecdote, the overheard snatch of conversation (mobile phones are a gift), the poem or the novel. I also have a soft spot for things that in themselves are stories. The process and evolution of a picture are part of its personality. A work might have gone through many phases of success and failure, testing and editing, clarification and mystery before it is settled, so storytelling in one form or another is the business of Art. Perhaps it all goes back to our ancient ancestors who sat around the fire repeating tales, scratching in the sand, singing songs to confirm and develop human experience.[41]

But even though he's failing to acknowledge vast swathes of both abstract and modern non-narrative art, the kind of narrative he is thinking of is 'ordinary narrative' as opposed to the 'strange and disturbing' narrative characteristic of art proper. And he makes clear the element of mysticism in

---

[41] Orr on the discerningeye.org website, (2016).

the process: '(Art) is the last bastion of an unreasonable world where intuitive feeling trumps all the myriad orthodoxies... contradiction is at the heart of creativity. No open submission exhibition makes sense. It is the very surprising unpredictability that makes it both significant and entertaining.'

All this is simply to point out the distinction between gallery going for aesthetics, and gallery going for art. Art is not about aesthetic mysticism and image fixation; it is about narrative congruence, and so it demands an entirely different approach to the presentational material. Aesthetics requires close reading of the aesthetic features, so it requires standing in front of the crafted works for long periods of time, studying the detail and hoping for moments of rapture; whereas art is about tuning in to the mindset behind the works, and inhabiting it as best you can. In the case of a Joseph Beuys exhibition, for example, there is the pleasure in being surrounded by the weird artefacts of an old and highly eccentric character, in the same way that it would be to visit the house of an old eccentric; but there is not much to be gained by close reading of each item, because it's not the detail which counts, it is the overall experience. Of course there is no law against close reading if it's what you want to do, but it's vaguely pointless, like studying a movie frame by frame instead of following the unfolding story and exploring its implications.

Artworks as 'relics'[42]

If we shift our focus from aesthetic detail to art narrative, it might seem as if gallery going is thereby devalued, because art is not to be found in a direct sensual encounter with the artworks, but in some sort of mysterious realm 'offstage'. In other words, it might appear as if 'art' could just as easily be revealed through photographs – or some other mediated access – as through gallery going. Aesthetic art, despite digital advances, still requires direct sensual contact with the original – or an indistinguishable copy – because any form of mediation, such as a photographic or video recording, cannot be substituted for the wealth of aesthetic information afforded by direct experience. And even if we assume that virtual reality can accurately replicate the contact with an item of aesthetic presentational crafting, we would still need to compare it with the actual experience to be sure of its accuracy, and

---

[42] For another take on this, see Noë (2014).

this somewhat defeats the purpose of the virtual replication in the first place; except of course in those instances where direct contact is practically impossible.

This brings us on to the idea of the aesthetic object – the classical painting or the sculpture – as some sort of secular relic, to be revered for its singularity, and not to be thought of as mechanically reproducible[43], or in any way replaceable. This makes sense insofar as aesthetics focuses on our direct sensorial experience of the unique features of crafted objects, and insofar as these objects have specific qualities that need to be experienced directly to achieve their full aesthetic effect. This means that while mediated contact with an important aesthetic object – say through photographs, video, or digital reproductions – is acceptable in the absence of the real thing, it is then perfectly meaningful to cherish the crafted object with a measure of reverence bordering on a type of religious devotion. The original crafted object unavoidably becomes something of a relic, even if it can be copied down to the last detail.

Art objects can be treated differently. While they certainly have contextual importance – such as historical value – individual artworks are never so crucial to the art experience as to be irreplaceable, because the art experience is located in an imaginative, narrative realm, and so once brought into being is not dependent on the existence of particular crafted items, no matter how iconic they might have become. It doesn't matter which exact urinal was the one chosen by Duchamp – any similar one will do – and this applies to the prints and photographs of Andy Warhol, or the constructions of Joseph Beuys. If some Gilbert and George photo-mosaics were destroyed in a fire, they could be replaced by copies without loss – no one knows, or cares, which is the original, or which was the 'first'.

And as it happens, some interesting and important modern artworks have already been lost to posterity, and can only be found in photographs. Joseph Beuys's iconic 'Fat Chair', and his 'Fat Corner' have decayed beyond repair, but their message lives on, and in a peculiar way the photographic record of their existence has a kind of poignant, nostalgic power of its own. Once again, it is the 'Beuys world' which is important, and where the 'art' is to

---

[43] Compare also the ideas expressed in the famous but difficult essay by Walter Benjamin 'The Work of Art in the Age of Technological Reproducibility' (2008) – and regularly anthologised in books of art essays. Benjamin, like John Berger (1997), was more interested in politics than in art, and his writings on art are oddly uninformative.

be located; it is not all about the integrity of the individual artworks.

Artworks, and their display in galleries

Once again, it might seem as if our devaluing of the singularity of individual artworks means that there is hardly any point in gallery-going at all, and that one could just as well connect with an artistic narrative through books and videos and other media. While this is true up to a point, the display of artworks in galleries has its own logic and its own value, though as we have seen, this is quite different from that relating to aesthetic objects.

There is obviously the question of size, and scale, and the composition of the artwork to be taken into consideration when it comes to gallery display; and these factors might prohibit the artwork being hung on a wall in a home, except in a mediated form. Transforming the size of a two-dimensional artwork can dramatically alter its impact, depending on what effect the artist wanted to achieve to begin with: standing in front of a 6 x 6 metre poster is a quite different experience from glancing at a reproduction in a book; and although any particular impact is incidental to the grasping of the art itself, it still has its own dramatic value.

The most important effect an art gallery can achieve is obviously that of immersing the viewer in a particular narrative, in such a way that the narrative achieves an extensiveness and richness which would be difficult under other circumstances. And at least a part of realising this narrative extensiveness would be dependent on the skill of the curator, in bringing together the right pieces in the right combination, and so either intensifying the narrative itself, or revealing new avenues within its possibilities.

Understanding Modern Art

16

OVERVIEW - ART & OUR PSYCHOLOGICAL LIFE - WHERE DOES ART FIT IN ?

In an earlier section we discussed the fact that currently – early 21st century – art is still a somewhat marginal pursuit, and most people, including those who go to galleries and exhibitions, only have the vaguest idea either of what they are looking for, or what they might be looking at. Generally speaking, cultural activities are seen as a civilised and perhaps worthy way to spend the occasional afternoon or evening; and culture is something you experience by gentle osmosis – it's your attendance at events which counts, not the extent of your active engagement – and all in all you don't have to think too much about it. Most people are content to leave the detail, and the sorting out of ideas, to the art professionals, and are only really interested in art in a very casual sense.

And we also need to repeat, once again, that many practicing artists themselves – including famous names - have only a very shallow and confused idea as to what 'art' might be 'in itself'. Because being a practitioner of a skill or discipline does not necessarily entail any real understanding of what it is you do, and in this regard artists often have no more to say on art than any relatively educated person, and artists regularly rely on clichés and stock phrases to explain themselves. Books 'about art' by artists and gallerists and critics testify to this; see for example, Salle (2018), Muir (2012), and Thornton (2009).

It may be that with increased leisure time, more people will take a more serious interest in art, and want to go beyond a casual and confused understanding of what art has to offer. This book has been about the first step on that path, in that it has sought to draw a clear distinction between 'art' and 'aesthetics', and to show how art proper is about a very specific type of narrative disclosure, in which 'strange and disturbing' realms of the imagination are presented to us for contemplation in a vicarious and recreational way. If 'art' and 'aesthetics' are confused – as they invariably are – then art never really tells us anything, and never really discloses to us its interesting narratives, because we are constantly being misdirected by discussions of aesthetic detail. You can't possibly understand the art of even major figures such as Beuys or Warhol or Koons if you try to analyse the physical features of their artworks; it is like trying to understand music by studying the physical constituents of various musical instruments.

But supposing we achieve a clear understanding of art: where does it get us ? How is it an improvement over the sort of enjoyable incomprehension that one feels when going into a gallery filled with bewildering artworks ? Isn't at least half the point of art the fact that no one knows what it is, and that, for once, anything goes ? Doesn't clarity and clear-headedness spoil all the fun ? No it doesn't: being able to connect with art in its own realm is more rewarding and satisfying than having to rely on trivial thoughts about how much a work is worth in monetary terms, or asking vague questions about 'meaning', or liking or disliking colours and shapes. Art has a real story to tell, and being able to connect with it is much more fun than hopping from one poorly-informed idea to another.

How far can art take us ? What is its furthest reach ? Mysticism aside, art is, as we have said repeatedly, a form of recreation, a form of secular contemplation. It is a worldly form of consciousness altering, in the sense that one enters into congruence with the mindset of another, but it does not require trance states or any kind of loss of everyday connectivity. Art is always deliberately vicarious and theatrical, always presenting crafted material at one remove from reality, even in those instances where it wants to be as immersive as possible.

There are those who want to use artworks – or creative presentational material – for purposes other than vicarious contemplation, and there is no good reason why this should not be done, except for the fact that, as soon as certain boundaries are crossed, it no longer remains art, but instead becomes something else. Very often a single piece of crafted material can be used for several purposes at one and the same time, and this contributes to the confusion in people's minds as to what exactly art is, but from our perspective as soon as a crafted work loses its position as an object of vicarious narrative contemplation, it loses its status as art. Warhol showed us how to use advertisements for artistic narrative, but identical images could also have functioned to get people to buy products.

Put simply, art which is not about vicarious contemplation and recreation is not art. Political posters are not 'art', they are craftings for political causes; religious statuary and imagery is not art, they are craftings whose purpose is mystical contemplation; activist art is not art, it is designed to get people to support social causes. But then what unique purpose does art have, if we separate it from all these other possibilities ? In itself, art can never be more than a type of entertainment, and a recreational diversion; a form of 'enjoyment' whose purpose is enjoyment itself. You engage with art to relax and enjoy yourself in the art; and that's it. Art won't solve the problems of the world, or take us closer to God, or make us better people; you'll need other things to do that.

This doesn't mean to say that the ideas that might flow from an engagement with art can't be put to all kinds of practical uses, but simply to say that 'art as art' is not about looking for ideas which have practical value. If you want ideas of practical value, then go to something practical, and get your ideas from there. If you want religious absorption and mystical states, go to religion; if you want to change the world, go into politics or social activism.

If you watch quintessentially art films like 'Last Year at Marienbad'(1961), or 'The Killing of the Sacred Deer'(2017), or 'Eraserhead'(1977), you can easily understand that they don't contain practical dimensions to them in the sense of urging the audience to adopt a specific course of action, or take on a specific ideology. They are essentially recreational 'entertainments', disclosing disturbing aspects of life in an entertaining way, such that we can contemplate these uncanny elements in a safe environment, both physically and mentally. They may provide us with ideas that we can apply in our everyday lives, but that is not their primary purpose, and to the extent that they stray into practical matters or into preaching, they are likely to weaken the impact of the art itself.

Then how does 'art' fit into life itself ? As we have seen from the hierarchical schemas based on Maslow, art is part of our reflective and contemplative capacities, near the top of the pyramid in psychological importance, yet very much dependent on more primitive needs having first been met. Art, as opposed to aesthetic crafting, requires a measure of societal stability and prosperity and individual freedom before it can manifest itself, in that it offers an advanced form of recreational contemplation not open to people who are in any way struggling for survival. This does not mean you have to be wealthy to create and appreciate art, but it does mean that societies under the threats of war, famine or disease will not have either the resources or the desire to engage with art, though they may well feel it necessary to expend much energy on other forms of aesthetic and decorative crafting.

Art is essentially a form of entertainment, and we use presentational crafting to enhance our enjoyment of life, and to satisfy psychological needs which cannot be responded to - or met - in any other way. It is not possible to explain our relationship to art in any simpler terms without descending into mysticism of one kind or another, or reducing art to something other than itself.

DEFINITION OF ART CHECKLIST

the crafted stuff we create and which surrounds us in our lived world can be divided into two major categories:

- **tools & implements**
  for surviving and thriving
  (everything from shoes to computers to sports kits)

- **presentational material**
  for recreation and reflection and decoration
  (artworks, books etc).

And non-utilitarian and presentational material can be further divided into three major categories:

- **aesthetic material**:
  decorative and beautiful objects

- **art**:
  narrative and disclosing objects
  Narrative material can be of two kinds:
  ordinary (diversionary entertainment) or
  artistic (strange and disturbing)

- **spiritual and philosophical written and spoken material**

BIBLIOGRAPHY

Acton, Mary. *Learning to Look at Modern Art*. Routledge, 2010.

Arnason, H. H., and Elizabeth C. Mansfield. *History of Modern Art*. Laurence King Publishing, 2012.

Bann, Stephen. *Interpreting Contemporary Art*. Harper Collins, 1991.

Barrett, Terry Michael. *Why Is That Art?: Aesthetics and Criticism of Contemporary Art*. Oxford University Press, 2017.

Benjamin, Walter, et al. *The Work of Art in the Age of Its Technological Reproducibility, and Other Writings on Media*. The Belknap Press of Harvard Univ. Press, 2008.

Berger, John. *Ways of Seeing: a Book*. British Broadcasting Corporation, 1977.

Bills, Mark. *The Art of Satire: London in Caricature:* Philip Wilson Publishers, 2006.

Canaday, John. *What Is Art?* Knopf, 1980.

Carroll Noël. *Theories of Art Today*. University of Wisconsin Press, 2000.

Chusid, Irwin. *Songs in the Key of Z: the Curious Universe of Outsider Music*. Chicago Review Press, 2000.

Cottington, David. *Modern Art: a Very Short Introduction*. Oxford University Press, 2005.

Dachy, Marc. *Dada: the Revolt of Art*. Thames & Hudson, 2006.

Davies, Stephen. *Definitions of Art*. Cornell Univ. Press, 1991.

Freeland, Cynthia A. *But Is It Art?: an Introduction to Art Theory*. Oxford University Press, 2002.

Greenberg, Clement, and John O'Brian. *Clement Greenberg: the Collected Essays and Criticism (Several Volumes)*. University of Chicago Press, 1995.

Greenberg, Clement. *Art and Culture: Critical Essays*. Beacon Press, 2006.

Harries, Karsten. *The Meaning of Modern Art: a Philosophical Interpretation*. Yale Univ. Press, 1991.

Heller, Nancy. *Why a Painting Is like a Pizza a Guide to Understanding and Enjoying Modern Art*. Princeton University Press, 2002.

Hughes, Robert. *The Shock of the New*. Alfred A. Knopf, 2013.

Hunter, Sam, et al. *Modern Art: Painting, Sculpture, Architecture*. Harry N. Abrams, 1992.

Krauss, Rosalind E. *Bachelors*. MIT Press, 2001.

Kuspit, Donald B. *The End of Art*. Cambridge University Press, 2008.

Lamarque, Peter, and Stein Haugom Olsen. *Aesthetics and the Philosophy of Art the Analytic Tradition: an Anthology*. Wiley Blackwell, 2019.

Maslow, A. H. "A Theory of Human Motivation." *Psychological Review*, vol. 50, no. 4, 1943, pp. 370–396., doi:10.1037/h0054346.

Menzies, Michael. *Deeply Superficial Noel Coward, Marlene Dietrich, and Me*. Magnus Books, 2012.

Muir, Gregor. *Lucky Kunst: the Rise and Fall of Young British Art*. Aurum, 2012.

Noë, Alva. "Are Works Of Art Relics?" *NPR*, NPR, 18 July 2014, www.npr.org/sections/13.7/2014/07/18/332405357/are-works-of-art-relics?t=1594296592085.

Orr, Chris. *The Discerning Eye - 2016 Exhibition - Chris Orr RA*, 2016, discerningeye.org/archive/2016/2016_9.php.

Pater, Walter. *The Renaissance; Studies in Art and Poetry*. London, Macmillan, 1910. B. Blackwell, 1973.

Salle, David. *How to See: Looking, Talking, and Thinking about Art*. W. W. Norton & Company, 2018.

Shore, Stephen, and Lynne Tillman. *Factory - Andy Warhol*. Phaidon Press, 2016.

Stallabrass, Julian. *Contemporary Art: A Very Short Introduction*. Oxford University Press, 2006.

Stecker, Robert. *Artworks: Definition, Meaning, Value*. Pennsylvania State Univ. Press, 1997.

Thornton, Sarah. *Seven Days in the Art World*. Granta, 2009.

Ward, Ossian. *Ways of Looking: How to Experience Contemporary Art*. Laurence King Publishing Ltd, 2018.

Wittgenstein, Ludwig, and G. E. M. Anscombe. *Philosophical Investigations = Philosophische Untersuchungen*. Blackwell, 2001.

Zaaiman, Jakob. "Jeff Koons: A Certified Extra-Terrestrial." *Artzine*, 2019, artzine.com/articles/jeff-koons-a-certified-extra-terrestrial.

Understanding Modern Art

INDEX

Abramović, Marina 87
abstract art 78, 103, 104, 108, 127-129, 146
activism (art) 19, 84, 85, 86, 120, 135, 136, 152, 153
Ai Weiwei 19, 102

Bacon, Francis 45, 111-113, 116, 119, 121, 138
Banksy 19
Barrett, Terry 21, 157
Beuys, Joseph 17, 45, 68, 69, 74, 102, 115, 119-121, 147, 148, 152
Bible 85
Bohemianism (artistic) 5, 58, 59, 63, 64, 130
Bosch, Hieronymus 31
Boulé, Michelle 133
Brahms, Johannes 45
Brancusi, Constantin 45
Breugel, Pieter 31

Calder, Alexander 46
Chusid, Irwin 133, 134, 157
curating (art) 71-73, 74, 75, 107, 111, 121, 135, 149

Da Vinci, Leonardo 52, 53
Dachy, Marc 105, 157
Dada 105, 106, 109, 139, 157
Decorative crafting 12, 26, 34, 43-46, 50, 60, 70, 71, 83, 88, 103, 115, 128, 129, 153, 155
Dickie, George 21
Duchamp, Marcel 71, 74, 105-109, 148

Emin, Tracey 102, 124, 126, 127
Explanation of art, an 4, 6-8, 25, 27, 69, 96, 106, 108, 120

Fauvism 31
Fountain (Duchamp) 71, 105, 107

Gilbert and George   125, 137, 148
Gillray, James   31
Greenberg, Clement   103, 128, 158

Hirst, Damien   117, 124, 125
Hollander, Xaviera   133
Hughes, Robert   138, 139, 145, 158

Impressionism   28, 30, 47
Incorrect music (genre)   133-135

Kooning, Willem de   104
Koons, Jeff   102, 115, 117, 121, 125, 137, 152, 159
Krauss, Rosalind   142-144, 158
Kuspit, Donald   37, 158

Lascaux Caves   25, 26
Lunch, Lydia   127
Lynch, David   45, 103

Manet, Edouard   28
Maslow, Abraham   39 -41, 42, 48, 49, 83, 153, 158
Mitchell, Joan   104, 105
Mona Lisa   52-54, 68
mysticism (art)   16, 37, 43, 45, 48, 64, 65, 84, 86, 120, 127, 137, 141, 146, 147, 152, 153

Nadar, Felix   30
Neoclassical   28

Orr, Chris   145, 146, 158

Paris   28-31
Pater, Walter   1, 158
Phenomenology   21, 22
Philosophy   7, 8, 19, 21, 22, 47, 61, 62, 88, 108, 158
Picasso, Pablo   11, 30, 103, 104, 129, 130
political art   19, 29, 47, 50, 55, 84, 85, 86, 107, 120, 121, 135, 136, 148, 152, 153
Pollock, Jackson   17, 45, 104, 127, 128

Raphael   17
realism   30, 47
Refusés (Salon de)   28-30
Ryman, Robert   129
Sewell, Brian   145
Shakespeare, William   63
Sherman, Cindy   142-144
Soviet   47
Spielberg, Steven   103
Spirituality   12, 41-43, 45, 50, 61
Sprinkle, Annie   127
Stalinist   34, 47
Stallabrass. Julian   15, 159
Stecker, Robert   20, 159
Strange & disturbing (art characteristic)   3, 45, 68, 79-83, 87, 89, 91, 93, 95, 102, 104, 105, 108, 109, 112-114, 118, 119, 121, 123-126, 130, 132-134, 137, 142, 146, 152, 155

Tartars   120
Television   12, 70, 138
Testino, Mario   111
Thatcher, Margaret   111
theatrical   34, 70, 71, 82, 83, 88, 107, 114-116, 119-121, 137, 152

urinal (Duchamp)   71, 105-107, 124, 148
utilitarian   26, 33, 43, 44, 50, 51, 54, 62, 64, 70, 73, 82, 106, 140

Velazquez   112
video   12, 14, 44, 72, 125, 145, 147, 148, 149
Viking   12, 51
vitrines   124

Warhol, Andy   45, 81, 97, 114-117, 119, 121, 132, 137, 148, 152, 159
Weitz, Morris   21
Wikipedia   105
Witkin, Joel-Peter   111
Wittgenstein, Ludwig   94, 159

YouTube   53, 72, 125, 139

Zaaiman, Jakob   117, 159, 162

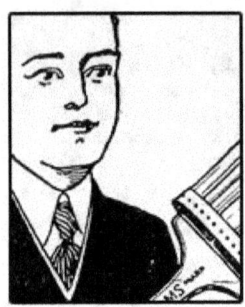

ABOUT THE AUTHOR

Jakob Zaaiman is an artist and writer living in London. He has written extensively on how best to understand modern contemporary art. He has a number of university degrees.

www.ingramcontent.com/pod-product-compliance
Lightning Source LLC
Chambersburg PA
CBHW071403210526
45465CB00001B/223